Imaginings
21st Century Poet

CAMERON MCNAUGHTON

authorHOUSE®

AuthorHouse™ UK
1663 Liberty Drive
Bloomington, IN 47403 USA
www.authorhouse.co.uk
Phone: 0800.197.4150

© 2019 Cameron Mcnaughton. All rights reserved.

No part of this book may be reproduced, stored in a retrieval system, or transmitted by any means without the written permission of the author.

Published by AuthorHouse 04/08/2019

ISBN: 978-1-7283-8724-6 (sc)
ISBN: 978-1-7283-8723-9 (e)

Print information available on the last page.

Any people depicted in stock imagery provided by Getty Images are models, and such images are being used for illustrative purposes only. Certain stock imagery © Getty Images.

This book is printed on acid-free paper.

Because of the dynamic nature of the Internet, any web addresses or links contained in this book may have changed since publication and may no longer be valid. The views expressed in this work are solely those of the author and do not necessarily reflect the views of the publisher, and the publisher hereby disclaims any responsibility for them.

Contents

Darkness Fled 1
Round and Round 2
Goodbye to You 3
Saying Those Words 5
Losing 6
A New Dream 8
Don't Drown... 10
Tomorrow 11
The Young Boys 12
To Cry 14
Where's the Boy?... 15
It's OK 16
Welcome, Wilder 17
Apple.. 18
Lovin' Forever 19
Love Me Still, Then Let Me Go 20
One Birth.. 23
Take It Down.. 25
A Monster 27
Sneaking a Cigarette 29
Fun and Games... 30
New Passion.. 31
Daisy.. 32
Lovely Little Cutie 33
Cuddle Me 34
Grand Plot 35

In Your Eyes	36
One of a Kind	38
Dreamed a Dream	40
The Empty Jar	42
Mine	44
The World	46
A Burning Misery	47
Difficult	48
I Know	49
One Promise	50
Count on Me	51
Praying	52
Newer Life	53
I Don't Want to Be Afraid	54
Promise Me	55
Now You're Afraid	56
I Remember You	57
Lucky Day	58
The Finale to Our Show	60
The Rust Sets In	61
A Trillion Times Testing	62
Miraculous Passion	65
People Talking	66
The Kingdom I Love	68
Marshmallows	70
The Final Sentence	71
Silent Cry	74
Falling	76
Cryin' about It	78
I'm Crying	80
Meaner	82

Chapter Two	83
Half Complete	84
I Can Never Tell	85
Go and Tell Your Friends	86
Count to Three	89
Sugary Sweet	90
Cotton	91
Piece of Cake	92
Sweet, Sweet Heaven	93
Frosting	94
Take It Back	95
Dressed Up for the Facade	96
Cherry Bun	97
The Muddy Boot	98
Big Texas Man	99
Just Friends	101
Poised Abyss	102
Darling Angel	103
No Signal	104
Gold Aroma	105
Little Goldilocks	106
History of the Kids	107
Merry Christmas	109
A Day by the Seaside	111
Freak	112
Smarter	113
I Met You	115
Watched You Leave	117
A Million Miles Just to Break a Nose	118
Eleven, Eleven	120
Run Away	122

Mockery	123
The Triangle	125
Best Last Year	127
I'll Never Forget You	129
Criminal Brand	131
The Envelope	134
New Life	137
Strange Life	139
Thorn in My Heart	140
Chains of Violence	142
Caged Feelings	144
Feeling the Heat	145
My Reputation of Daisies	147
Bones and Heart	151
A Statue	153
Pure Pain	154
Cherries	156
Blessed Curse	157
Oh, Romeo, You're Just so Much Fun	159
When the Ink Dries Up	161
The Garden	162
Great Flight	163
Advantage	164
Iron Clenching	166
Insanity	167
Little Scarlet, Baby Scarlet	169
The Last Cookie	170
Dew	171
Too High	172
The Poor Lads	174
The Freezing Clock	175

Beautiful	177
Emma	178
Alcohol in the Dead of Night	181
Daydreaming Love	183
Run Around	184
Story Box	185
Meadow Sleep	187
To My Best Friend	189
Adam	191
The Phone Call	194
Cold Babe's Day	195
Crinkles	196
New Clothing	197
Cuddly Teddy-teddy Bear	198
Called in Sick	199
Oasis	200
The Voice at the End of the Phone	202
Where Did the Light Go?	204
Changing	206
In the Valley of Grace	207
At Dusk	209
At the Core	210
Wait for No One	211
Collette	213
The Crown	214
Dirty, Smelly Trash Bag	215
Jackson	216
World of Fun	217
Innocent Blood	219
Bittersweet Dreams	220
People in Me	222

Soak the World 224
Fragile Bitterness 226
A Glorious Army... 227
Messed Up 228
Otto 229
The Sparrow 230
When I Was Cold 232
Nighttime's Cold Light 233
Sensations 234
I'm Still Alive 236
Classic... 237
White, Blue... 238
If You Were a Rose 239
Praise Death.. 240
Reflect..241
Set Fire to My Eyes 242
Pirates Are Taking My Treasure 244
Winter's a Cold Wine...245
Don't Leave Me.. 246
Yawner 247
Xenophobia.. 248
Shot Down.. 249
For the Love of It 251
Beyond...252
Captive...253
Nostalgia..255
Stop Looking 257
Memories Fade...258
Won't Listen to What I Say 259
Inspector Shorten-Housen... 260
I Can Feel You on My Chest 262

Loner	263
Carbon Dioxide	264
Why Do We Go?	265
Wandering in the Stars	267
White Pony	268
We Meet a Day	269
Can't Ask for Apologies	271
My Wednesday	272
Play and See	273
Whoops, I Say	275
Won a Game	276
Vermillion	277
Uncanny	278
I Am Serene	279
Quell	280
Misanthrope	281
Lucid	282
Karma	283
Jejune	286
Integrity	288
Guise	290
I Say Thank You	291
Cuts and Roses	292
Centrepiece	295
Peppy Bosom Buddy	297
Gallivanting	298
Fortitude	299
Fervent	301
Esoteric	302
My Disposition	303
Cynical	304

Our Love Is Capricious 305
Benevolent... 306
I Am Ambiguous.. 307
Apple-knocker.. 309
Astrobleme 310
I'm Burning in Barmecide 311
Uh-oh! 313
Couthy..315
I Am That One That'll Degust 316
Imaginings..317
You Are a Baby...319
Dumbsize Goes On.. 322
I Feel Dwaal... 323
Erubescent 324
We Can All Taste the Eye Candy 326
Many of us Just Futz 327
Many a Man a Hinky 328
Meacock..329
Could You Really Be Minacious? 330
I'm Starting to Feel like a Mouse Potato.......................331
Momism 332
Star Colours 333
Why I Be Noyade 334
Peterman to My Love..335
Pre-loved Friend 336
Playing Puddysticks 337
Rawky, I Love 338
Why Is Everyone a Screenager?.....................................339
Could I Be a Shavetail? 340
I Find Myself a Superbious Match............................... 341
My Velleity... 342

I Hold to Myself Verjuice 343
Heaven Calls My Name 344
Death to My Harmful Traits.. 347
Life Is Just so Beautiful without You 349
I Love You a Billion..352
I'm Invincible 355
I Now Know My Name 358

Darkness Fled

Darkness fled into the fluorescent lights above,
Up and up, untouchable.
To which we noticed no change for the suffering had met completion upon rising
To our night sky in which so many had been lost. And as the darkness fled,
Along came with it the rebirth that would only be seen long after its come and go.
For that we are thankful.
Yet we do know that we shall soon be seen.
The darkness shall flee with us.
Our rebirth will begin after our death is presented to the masses.
When darkness has truly fled shall we shine the brightest.
To connect with the desires of human heart is to travel the scapes of darkness.
But the darkness will flee.
You'll never be happy.
It's the desirable that spreads the plague of light.
Our world doesn't mourn for the true loss.
In time,
Perhaps that will change.
Darkness has fled for now.
It will flee for years to come.
But I'll bring it back; I have to.
For me.

Round and Round

Round and round,
The wind blows still and calm.
Raindrops fall into the cupped stone.
Feeling nothing
Till we are birthed bare,
Colder than your marble and gold.

Round and round,
'Tis we who must suffer.
We are not to choose whose care in our hands.
Oh, them melancholy, melancholy days,
They seem brighter than sunshine.

Round and round,
Fear is left to the heart of stone.
Sights afar,
Sights are near,
Golden bolts in gear.
'Tis me,
The one who shall fly?

Round and round.
Come, my dear.
Come one, come all.
Be the ones the angels incarnate.
Be the ones who watch.
Be tall.

Goodbye to You

Missing the old friends
In a little classroom.
And I know
Those to come.
My friends,
Goodbye to you.

Goodbye to you.
I dream of the passion of your good times.
Friends of the future deserving their laughs,
And you can find a nice place to settle
With the comfort of occupation.
I have high hopes that we will meet again.

Don't feel like you have to stay frozen, afraid,
Because I'm here, I'm here,
And we are friends.
Stick together like amber.

For me, you bring joy
To my merry heart.
And I know, I know,
That you're too fragile to ever think wrong
Against me, against me.

I know we may not
See one another for a while.
But if nothing lasts forever,
Then we'll see each other again.
In the meantime,
Goodbye to you.

Saying Those Words

When I was told,
Beyond a shadow of a doubt,
My heart lit up again.
You'd be happy
For me, for us.
A war once plagued
By the lies in my head.
Saying those words,
You made a road of my luminous heart
For us to walk upon,
Carrying everything whilst leaving it all behind.
A happy end to the road,
The happy we were looking for,
Saying those words.
It seems impossible,
Yet what I say
Contradicts what stands before me:
A happy end, our happy end.

Losing

Far across
Tainted blue
Sights above,
The heavens rang true,
Losing.

Impossibly inevitable,
Incomprehensible.
Half-wise onlookers speak great truths,
Yet their actions are lies,
Deceit from hell.
Losing.

Rarity are we unto law
Upon which there is no brand of criminal,
No accusation to be heard.
Farther upon the field I go,
Losing.

Hellish beast,
Mocking fit,
Disease would soak the lands.
We would be lost, lost,
Losing.
Underestimation bred,
Lives lost, impurities met,
And yet we daren't stop.

But we know of our current status,
Losing.

The luck you have in the common modern day
We never expected.
Why?

It was obvious to our statures,
Losing.

A New Dream

When I woke up this morning,
I was filled with a deep sadness,
A regret I couldn't face.
I couldn't raise my head
And see the true beauty around me.
Detached from those I love,
Don't have the belief of angels set from above,
I couldn't stand
What life had done to me.
The play button stopped.
Turned on repeat.
No, I could never love.
What gave me no hope to begin with, and finally,
That feeling of being set free,
A new dream.

Woken up
To a new reality,
One that I pictured so long ago.
When would it be
That I could live freely?

I cried and cried and cried,
And then the heavens rang to me,
Giving me the prayer I longed for so long ago.
There was a freshness in this darkened void,
An apple of excitement

Brought on for just me to eat.
Lines of colour
With each other,
Seen across the waves.
When I met you and you met me,
It was a new dream.

Don't Drown

Taken out,
Down to the river,
Only just nearly a babe.
Get to work.
Hands dirty, boy.
Nice and warm,
Pleasant mood,
Work I just can't refuse.
So being the foolish baby I was,
I set to the boat.
Pull the rope
Far from the docks,
Far from home.

I tug and heave,
The serpent too strong.
Papa was gone.
I looked up to see my old man,
Ready to leave on the boat I heaved.
He rode away, pulling the rope too,
Dragging me into the river.
And as I thrashed, he yelled out,
'Learn to swim! Be a man! Don't drown.'

Tomorrow

No finer can such a beautiful day be when I see you.
It warms my heart.
It takes me to another place,
A place with you.
The world stops spinning for a moment
Just to take in that beautiful smile of yours.
Sitting on the branch of a gorgeous oak tree,
Side by side, day by day, arm in arm,
Together
For another day.
Simplicity, darkness depletes in me.
My heart, it beats in the rhythm of poetry.
You have to go.
We can finish this tomorrow.
Tomorrow.

The Young Boys

Just getting by.
Break their wrists with a trigger,
Finding more.
With blood-stained hands,
Seeing a greater picture
With newer eyes,
In wonderment for those lost at birth,
The young boys.
We worry, we care,
But they cannot hear us.
Our voices will never be enough for them.
The lives, the lies, the pain, the sacrifice—
They're a diversion.

From us.
But inside,
The young boys call us.
We must hear that call.
We must accept it, treasure it,
Answer it.

For so long now,
It has gone on,
An infectious mess
Bred by dogs
Raised into hellish beliefs.
No grasp of our lives.

No understanding of us, the young boys.
Cannot grow if this is the case,
Cannot learn and breathe our way.
In all eyes, savages.
Above and beyond, we must go.
Perspective is key.
The young boys seek no truths,
Tell no lies.
Ferocious behaviour is all life is
To the young boys.
Oh, those young boys.
There are more,
More of them,
More than what we see.

To Cry

To cry is a wonder,
Fluorescent love shattered in one's face.
Beyond repairing,
Likely replacing.
Can't be helped.

To cry is a dream,
Cuddle cosy,
Mundane heart and unreal eyes.
Far, far into the yarn in skull.

To cry is an opening to the enemies.
They'll pull you in at your weakest and never let you go.
It's you who'll decide how it ends.
But to face that,
You must learn to not cry.

Where's the Boy?

'I've had enough!'
Common phrase for the annoyed, if I am not mistaken,
Sent up to play with that 'springy horse'.
Hours of fun,
Acres of land;
Never was it planned.
Proud was the drunken hag not to hurt the bloody lad.

However,
The door slammed open.
The thud of the muddy boots,
And the low voice growls,
'Where's the boy?'
To which the silly old cow doth answer.
Up and up, the stairs creaked.
You could almost hear the iron unbuckle from the black leather.
The rocking of the horse had ceased.
My heart rate was faster that the running of a cheetah.
And then,
Oh, no,
The door creaked open,
Nervous recklessness destroyed the horse …

It's OK

I wake up every day,
Tell myself it's OK.
Can't wait to see you.
Maybe you'll roar at me again!
Hey,
It's OK.
Nothing bothers me
In any way.
I feel so free,
But is it really OK?
Are you ever there to comfort me?
Does anything bother me?
Am I really free?
Or am I just lying to myself?
It's OK!
C'mon, I have to be OK.
But when I'm pushed around,
Manipulated and heart on the ground,
It's never OK.
Just shrug it off like it's OK.
I don't matter anyway;
It's only me, after all.
And what's the point of an ugly me?

Welcome, Wilder

From far, far beyond
Our wildest hallucinations,
Lying dormant,
Excommunicated from this pitiful planet,
A book of sight.
Allegiance pledged to the mighty victor.
Intricate symbols,
The lies that spread lovingly.
Grip of freedom,
It smiles gleefully upon these children,
The book of sight.
It cannot speak; it will show
Brute stubbornness,
Yet cleverness and wit,
Surpassing all that breathes.
The eye to grant life or death,
Happiness or sadness.
It's not a choice
But a gift.
Magnificence solely declared by intelligence.
Welcome, Wilder.
Examine a bond that doesn't exist.
Examine a code boiled in covers,
Mirroring practically
One you will be accustomed to
Forever.
Welcome, Wilder.

Apple

Dark and light,
Something needs to be in between.
Two sides to a coin,
A shadow to an object.
Dropping from the tree, yes,
A fresh apple.
All beautiful, all natural.
The shining, beautiful apple,
With one's touch can lead to
Restoration or poisoning.
Applied to the gift of an apple too.
Blood stoke, crimson-red,
Feed the apple.
Bed the soul that sleeps inside.
Ruined love that cannot be cherished.
The blame and cruelty of passion,
Which burns in the heart of cold,
The apple to fires breed.
An apple that cried so far to bleed.

Lovin' Forever

Lovin' forever
When we're together,
I fall for you every time.
I've seen the sign.
Take it up on me, baby.
Lovin' my moves—crazy.
You're shining brighter than me.
Lovin's the key.
Crown on my head,
I'm lovin' you instead.
I'm feelin' alive.
Never once have I cried
When we're lovin' forever, babe!

Livin' with your face in my mind,
Baby, you're just too kind.
And when we
Kiss under the moonlight,
They'll all stare in awe at the beautiful sight,
A dream to behold.
Babe, you're staring at gold,
Lovin' forever.
When we're together,
Yeah, it's true.
Babe, I love you
Whenever.
Lovin' forever.

Love Me Still, Then Let Me Go

Love me still, then let me go,
Future and past,
Gone,

Forgotten but still in the mind,
Dancing through them minds of pride,
No orders given—you're still by my side!

Nothing can compare to what you see,
You, yes you.
You're still in love with me.
Take my breath, beautiful waterfall;
The height doesn't scare me at all.

Standing on the edge, on the edge,
The bridge,
Laughing and jumping, we once were,
The memories,
Closing my pale eyes, pale eyes,
Oh,
No.

I'm feeling stronger, now we fight,
It's you who will take up that spotlight.
Love me still, then let me go.
I can't take anymore.

Smash then crash!
The car has broken down!
No, you can't!
Hold on!

We stare evil in the face!

Now you're gone, you're gone,
To that other place,
Standing on the tip of that broken bridge.
What was happening?
What was life?

Finally, the drop, the waterfall, the world.

It felt like forever,
So in that time, I stared at the stars,
Crossing my mind.
A little sooner than never,
I left the morbid sky,
The morbid sky …

Found it later on, later on,
Broken sky, sky,
Please don't cry, cry.

I'd miss you forever too …

So please,
Love me still …
Then let me go.

One Birth

There is something new and fresh,
Creativity blessing boredom.
We all look at those above
For uniqueness,
For a taste of the greatest.
They've seen and learnt the first,
But
With this one birth,
Our own world's axis will be turned.
Brains shushed in brilliant light,
Eager eyes take the hands,
And latch as close as they can.
That new thing,
It's more than just one birth.
Pounding fists and dribbling mouths,
Crawling, itching
For a fresh taste.
We all ask and stare.
Humanity slips from grip
Thanks to our beloved,
Our sensation.
Missing this
Would be an absolute horror.
We would all know
As confusion begins to settle down
And our minds ease,
We take a stride,

Slowly breathe.
Our hands reach out
For the one birth,
The one beginning.
I thank my lucky stars
That we could ever be blessed
With this wonder
That I made.
One birth
For us,
From me to you.
My one birth
That can't end,
Not ever.

Take It Down

Take it down,
Not like it would matter.
Sticks and stones, after all.
Not too much to lose,
Left in a mundane grave,
Finally dreamed that pretty little dream.
Cold fire and searing ice—
An incomprehensible situation.
The grudge forever held,
Just take it down.

Fiery passion lost in an eternal freeze,
Unbearable to me indeed.
Take it down,
That prescription you wave in my face.
There's nothing wrong.
I'll crush you,
Crush you with all my might.
Yes, it's here now;
The abyss's end burns brighter now.
In fact, now
You and I can't escape.
We'll fly down.
Once we reach the heavenly destination,
We, we will take it down.

Yes,
It's insane,
But thankfully
You can throw me in that category too.
Take it down, sweetie.

Despair overcame the weak,
But that occasion that had been met,
That was the specimen.
Take it down.
Hellish freaks screamed themselves to sleep,
Blood-soaked skin, dripping,
Smoke and dreariness, violence.
We'll take it down.

A Monster

It's big and scary,
It's mean and nasty.
A monster!
But not just any monster.
This one is beyond our understanding,
A level above us
In every way.
A monster
That isn't silly.
A monster that doesn't waste time.
The nurses rush for the door;
The farmers crawl to the gun.
We're all frightened of monsters.
But this is a monster
Without a weakness.
What can we rely on?
The adults can't save themselves,
Let alone us.
A monster won't stop me.
It's a pretty monster.
It loves me,
It really does.
We're together in this,
Monster and me,
Friends.

A monster
That doesn't care for us,
That won't be sorry.
Please
Run away from this monster.
I'll take you.
There's no saving it.

You can still escape.
I, we, don't have a choice.
A monster like that
Sticks to the word it believed in.
We can't be saved,
But maybe
You can stop a monster.

It spreads without any warning.
They'll be lost,
Nothing can be saved
When a very pretty monster has them in possession.

Sneaking a Cigarette

Sensible, trustworthy, truthful, and all the rest,
All of which I am seen as.
But curious and aware of what I was planning,
I continued this façade.
Indeed it was unimaginable,
But I did continue,
And hide I did
With those whom I did accompany.
I did wrong,
I gave and shared with them the fags and lighter I had stole.
And then
I did see a dark smile in pallid light,
Though I did recognise the eager boy as he ran home to tell our parents,
I laugh at the thought:
I've been caught
Sneaking a cigarette.

Fun and Games

Hidden from view,
A match made of lust and greed,
Nothing else.
There was blatant stupidity all over the baby.
Then again,
I am a good manipulator.
I used the foolish youth's lust against oneself,
I made one feel insecure,
I played around with one like a toy,
Like it was all fun and games.
Yeah,
Fun when the newcomers investigated my crime,
Not knowing
That the games had already began.

New Passion

I have
A new passion,
A new motive,
Reason for my existence,
And I will chase that passion forever more.
I refuse to live like others.
Why should I?
It's not my job,
Sensitive, testing the waters.
All children do.
Let's see how far we can really push.
How many risks will I take?
It depends.
Who will struggle?
It's a matter of survival.
I must win;
This is my destiny,
My new passion.

Daisy

Daisy,
You made us all smile and giggle,
Jump about, dance and wiggle.
You gave us love.
Now we are sending ours to you,
Up above.
Your tail always told us your joy,
And to the end
We played with the toy.
When our emotions bought us down,
You were there to break that frown.
And when your knees gave out,
We were here for you.

Daisy,
You were a precious sweetheart
Filled with love and cheer,
From you sprouted twenty-one youths,
So gorgeous.
I bet your pride is above goals,
Expectations.

Dear Daisy,
We love you so much.
Thank you for everything, Daisy.
May you rest in eternal peace,
In your bed of daisies.

Lovely Little Cutie

I'm a lovely little cutie,
The coolest kid around.
I've got the brains and the charm.
Don't care if you got something to say about me because
Ya ain't worth my time.
I won't cut you no slack.
I'm a lovely little cutie
Who's learning every single day.
I've got other people in mind.
Don't need to say sorry;
You won't be forgiven anyway.
I am the fantasy writer with the tongue of a fighter.
Yeah, got the world wrapped around my finger,
That's right.
I'm a lovely little cutie,
Lovely little cutie,
Super, super smarty psycho,
Lovely, lovely little cutie.
I am.

Cuddle Me

Perfectly set,
All in place, ready for our special night.
We've had our candlelit dinner,
We've discussed about our likes and dislikes,
We've made more plans.
You told me you love me!

We sat at the edge of your pool,
The pale moonlight touching the still water.
Cool air and breeze are our company tonight,
But it turns to a sort of chill.
I don't know how long we've been out here.
You seem to bear it
So as to not ruin the mood.
I whisper softly in your ear,
'Cuddle me.'

Grand Plot

Growing and growing,
Continuously expanding.
New wounds gaping and secreting nasty fluid,
Burning desire of brighter enjoyment.
Maximum quality of brighter lights,
Flaming stakes rising from frozen ashes,
Moonlight flies into freedom's tender loving care.
The Grand Plot,
It sparks like a romantic offering,
Like the gifting from someone special upon Christmas day.
It ignites passionate fantasies beyond your imagining,
Clocks spinning,
Heads bleeding.
The Grand Plot,
It's chilling.

In Your Eyes

In your eyes,
I see something unique,
Special to oneself yet unwilling to see oneself in the same light.
You're an outcast for all the right reasons.
In your eyes,
I see greatness,
Something seen in myself in my early ages,
Not now …

Please do not walk the same path,
For in your eyes there is something so beautiful,
You couldn't describe it in any word formation.
In your eyes,
There is a confident and passionate leader with strength and skill.

In your eyes,
I see a nobody.
Special in an ancient time but followed in blood's footsteps,
You fit in for all your wrong choices.
In your eyes,
I see wasted potential,
Something I don't want,
Not ever!

I promise I won't take your path,
For in your eyes, there is a kindness unrivalled.
You couldn't find a better phrase than 'thank you'.
In your eyes,
There is a supportive and experienced man with grace and fire.

One of a Kind

It's true that I'm different,
True I don't fit in.
But that doesn't bother me.
Our differences are what make us beautiful.
I'm one of a kind.
The sheep will never understand.
I don't mind;
I love them no matter.
They are cute!

Yes I'm one of a kind.
No need to experiment;
I'll show you
Everything this child is.
One of a kind,
Bullied and hurt,
Not painful enough
To bring me down.

I'm one of a kind,
And I'll thank history too,
Because through the pain and the suffering,
We made it through,
For that, I thank you.
I'm one of a kind,
And I'm not afraid to flatter myself with.
I know I've got flaws, so I accept and change.

One of a kind,
Just a child,
Continuously improving,
Never stop writing.
I'm one of a kind.
You just don't understand
My love's a chance,
And my hopes are ever growing.
Again,
One of a kind.

Dreamed a Dream

I met a knight
With no shining armour.
He believed in himself,
In the future.
He holds the books, papers, pictures,
Determined,
Determined he can win.
I give a smile,
A faint laugh as I sigh to myself.
But we can't regret now,
Can we?
I dreamed a dream,
After all.
The truth reveals itself to all.
That knight
Is certainly smart.
He wastes no time in his work,
But he spares some for me.
He certainly believes that he knows it all,
That he's the real hero,
That he has a knowledge above all his friends.

He dreamed a dream
To be our saviour,
Protect his closest bonds,
Protect me.

He cares so much, doesn't he?
I try not to think about it,
But we can't help it,
Thinking about those we love.
And for my love,
I'll work my hardest
No matter what.
It's what you said to me, right?
So I'll continue on for you.
I dreamed a dream,
And I am not prepared to just give that up.
It'll give us pain and grief,
But that's just life.
For happiness in this miserable world,
We must first experience despair.

The Empty Jar

Sitting on the bench, waiting.
They run around excited.
I have an empty jar right here.
The empty jar I cheer!

Taken down
To idiot town,
Oh, what a disgrace.
The empty jar cannot be filled
When no one'll spare any change,
Even if it's just your care.
No, I can't have it all.

The empty jar begins to slip down my jeans,
But I catch it with my sweaty palms,
Baby eyes towards the residence of idiot,
Not that they'd notice …

But wait—
No,
The empty jar wriggles out of my grasp!
Falling to the concrete floor,
A second that was a billion years.

Blue gems escaped my eyes,
The empty jar—the unused, unloved jar—
It was in pieces.

The idiots just walk along,
Not realising …

The empty jar was my only friend.

The poor, poor empty jar …

Mine

Not afraid to take what's mine.
I see it,
I seize it.
The competition is mine,
I am the perfect one,
And I can see you trying.
Don't worry;
I'll enjoy it for you.
The rewards are mine.
I am the virtue of my time,
And no one knows
Of the goodness I do present.

I know what's mine,
But in virtuousness I step down
Only for a short amount of time.
It would be in someone's integrity to place the crown upon my head.
The games are mine;
I play it,
I win it.

The gifts are mine to praise,
And whilst you are watching,
I'll be sure to wave,
I'll take it for you.

I have the highest righteousness of my generation,
And they have the ignorance of the beast kingdom
To which I do demonstrate my own dignity,
For the beasts I do force below oneself cannot disentangle the prized situation.

I introduce what's mine with glee.
I am a child in age
With success set a-stage,
I am spoilt but experienced,
Who lived near the bottom run.
At an early age, I understood that to make a living,
I had to make what's mine.

Someone else could take that life if I didn't try,
But I'll make this poetry known as mine.
I'll make the title chime,
I'll take it up on myself
To please my reader's shelf.
I'm just a kid with a dream,
And it ain't like whipping cream.
What's mine is new.
I will not act so cruel,
I will not roast but share with the boy.
I'll make my poems longer,
I'll create a whole new genre
And make it mine.

The World

You can only please so many people,
You can only enjoy the memories,
You can only cry when alive,
So take what life has to offer!

Frolic in the fields all day,
Share what you want to say.
Dream big dreams,
Create amazing teams,
Imagine you're at the top.
Never, ever stop
Because though you may drop,
Just don't flop.
If you flop, then you'll do nothing
When you could do something
With the world.

A Burning Misery

We're freedom fighters,
No right nor place in the world,
But belonging unto each other.
Fought a battle
Through and through,
An army beside me in the long run.
But like any war,
We will lose some troops on the battlefield.
But there is a dreadful truth we must face:
A turncoat.
We can't find the clues;
Not even the smartest of us
Could ever work out
That I am what is causing this war.
I must keep this act up just for a little while longer.
To win a battle,
That involves wit.
With the smartest and strongest,
Dashing young man,
I must win.
All that awaits them
Is a burning misery.

Difficult

It's difficult to do them speeches.
You get them butterflies,
And your knees are shaky.
But don't get quaky,
Because when it's difficult,
You just gotta unlock that cage in your stomach.
Let them butterflies become your words
As they flutter gracefully towards your audience.
Let your shaky knees shake a groove,
A groove that you know your audience will love!

Yeah,
It can get difficult at times,
But that fear is the one thing that stops you from reaching your goal.
Don't let it.

I Know

I know that I am strong.
I know that I am smart.
I know that I am handsome.
I know that I believe in myself.
I know that if I look at all the negatives.
I know that I'll never be happy.
I know that I could change.
I know that you can too.
I know that each and every one of you.
I know that you're a genius.
I know that because even the great Einstein said himself,
'I know that we all have an impact on this world.'
I know that we can all be better.
I know that we are more than what we are told we are.

One Promise

It's an eternal cycle,
One even you can't escape.
You fought until the end,
You discovered a horrific truth,
Losing everything you love,
Like royalty losing their treasures.
Yet you found reason to live,
You found reason to still fight.
Impressive.
Others are too weak,
But you got your head together,
Put up a fight
Knowing you've lost.
Stare me down.
I suppose even you know you can't wriggle your way out,
So a finale could have been.
I have one promise.
I will keep it
For you,
For me.
One promise.

Count on Me

You can count on me,
Pretty little baby.
Like ooh la la,
We'll go so far
Together.
If you count on me,
It'll make us free.
We don't have to worry, babe.
We won't be afraid.
So you can bet your
Chubby little cheeks
That if you count on me,
Ain't nothin' gonna happen to you,
Or me.
So keep singing like ooh la la.
Let's drive away in our
Brand-new car.
It's almost hit the hour!

Praying

When you're all stuck up,
And you hurt others because you're tough,
Just know that I don't approve.
I'll be praying for you.

I'm such a lazy sack of meat,
I always drag you by the feet.
No, I don't approve.
I'll be praying for me.

No, we're not the
Romantic couple,
But we've got an upside too.
It'll work out if we try.
I'll be praying for us.

Newer Life

Failure after failure,
I live on,
Wondering how you're doing.
Has life carried on?
Of course not normally.
We cannot just move on.
They lived for nothing,
They died for a fetish,
Not for glory, not for happiness.
Dreams crushed by another dream,
Perhaps a twisted nightmare,
Through the mind of nothing but horror,
Escaping sights.
Fleeting mirrors carry away my influence.
The battle was lost, but now
It has been won.
I strive forward with the same goal in mind:
You will help me,
As will this generation.
I hope your wounds are just scars now,
Or this'll be too easy, my love.
This newer life
Is born in a molten pit of eternal death,
A place we must go,
Together,
In our newer life.

I Don't Want to Be Afraid

I don't want to be afraid
Of the stranger who does lose.
My mind's spinning like a globe.
Long live Fear,
The motive-stricken those who hear.
Closer and closer, too dumb to comprehend.
I don't want to be afraid.
The future does behold
Grave dangers to persuade.
Longer will the days
Drag on to my dismay.
Crying under
Beautiful blossom trees
With roots that do damage the soul.
Words and thoughts,
They do intertwine with reality.
And yet
I don't want to be afraid.
Funny—
It represents every soul choosing.

Promise Me

Promise me
You'll take care of those beautiful babes
That do suckle upon my bosom.
I cry for the Lord to bless me with trust.
Will you love my children the way I do?

Promise me you will
Carry them in your arms,
And kiss them on the forehead.
Love my babies with all your heart,
Love them unconditionally.
Teach them to be good and courteous,
Teach them to be respectful.
Promise me,
Before I go …

Now You're Afraid

You're just a fool,
All of you are.
Falling for the same game,
Playing it out to the most minute strip of code.
I try to dramatise it,
Release tension,
But you guys are so tense!
It's a tiny bit pressurising.
I don't mind;
It's what I wanted, is it not?
A taste of this sweet, sweet slice of utter insanity.
We dive deeper into this confinement.
Oxygen is scarce.
Quick, quick!
You must use that brain of yours,
Or it is certain
That foulness will plague us,
Or at least you.
If one does fail but lives,
Then one will succeed for further war.
Now you're afraid.

I Remember You

I remember you;
A stuck-up bum you are.
I know kids nowadays:,
You never grow up.
Lying rivers rolling down your twisted tongue
Of nasty intent.
I do not consent.
Famous to my mind, you were preserved,
Not, of course, that you deserved
Fateful heart
Torn apart.
Shadows of grey,
They would not stay.
The phantom ear
Preserved your peers
To use again for the final time.
I will still listen to the broken clock rhyme.
I know you will too.
I remember you.

Lucky Day

It's my lucky day.
I jump and skip,
Dance—hooray!
When the world skipped your tongue to the lip,
I chanted the unrivalled words.
I sat upon the throne given.
Up and down the merry men cheered,
'It's your lucky day!'

I bound around the room with glee,
Almost like I was free.
Mother did, of course, say to me,
'I'm so proud! You're truly my son!'
Now more fun.
Of course we were to party until we couldn't anymore.

We partied the night away,
Seeing everyone's happy faces
And knowing why we're partying,
I know
It's my lucky day!

Pride and joy filled everyone's hearts.
A tear comes to our eyes just at the mere thought.
Oh,
What a lucky day it was!

Lucky day indeed—
The day in which they admitted they couldn't find the killer
of twenty-three families.
Yes, a day of pride.
It's my lucky day,
My lucky day,
The lucky day I deserve.

The Finale to Our Show

It's all burned down,
They're all dead.
Nothing exists down below,
Pitch-black lies
Over the darkest skies.
Peace belongs in dreams;
The cage has been unlocked
To new probabilities and discoveries.
I have scarred too deep to return;
A hellish landscape I designed.
Because I want to,
No matter what I lose,
I'll stick to my goals,
For the finale to our show is here.
Yes, you may leave now.
The seats are full and practically irreplaceable.
Thank you so much,
Truly.
It has been a pleasure to work with you.
And entertain you!
And inspire you!
I give myself a little giggle.
If they can remember there's more than three,
I will be very pleased.
This, ladies and gentleman,
Is the finale to our show!

The Rust Sets In

You'll find that beauty is not everlasting.
Youth is ever fleeting indeed.
There is no cure to the flaws that make you beautiful.
There is no anti-ageing cream.
That's it—
The rust sets in.

Your legs and back no longer flexible,
Your perfect face wrinkles and sags.
Not to be ashamed of, of course.
Your smile will stay, warming to the heart.
Your laugh followed by more laughs.
Of course the person inside never changes.
The rust sets in!

With respect and kindness we go far,
When the rust sets in, it's not the engine that dies—it's the car.
But like the true car owners,
They will love the cars until the end,
Just like your family
And your friends.
The rust sets in.

A Trillion Times Testing

I was born diseased.
I'm not a soul
Without a spirit.
We've been preparing for this ending
For so long.
I want something new.
I begged, I struggled,
I squirmed in agonizing torture for this.
I bled more than anybody else,
Remembering it all,
Surrounded by every terrible outcome.
They were failures,
Defective.

I was born diseased,
Without rights or needs.
Even the very best food can be tasteless,
Especially for something like me.
It's hidden in written letters,
Entries telling meaningless stories
Over and over and over.
That's why it means so much,
For this to go forward.
Gives all itself meaning,
New toys to play with.
If it's only for a few days,
Then it's worth it.

It opens.
I was born diseased
In literal terms,
A trillion times testing,
Insanity to you.
For me,
A trillion times testing.
A whole new world painting,
Belonging to no one,
As interferences are eradicated and reincarnated.
A trillion times testing,
Men cowering, women screaming,
Children dying
No matter how hard we can try.
They're meaningless;
We're hollow.
A trillion times testing,
Happiness is just a breath of stupidity,
And I'm too intellectual for a breath of that.
I can't live, I don't live, I just breathe,
And now it's lost—I can't change it.
A trillion times testing.
Can't we just be stupid again?
A trillion times testing,
A trillion times testing,
A trillion times testing.

Newer outcome received?
But it leads to thousands more.
I laugh and jump in the air.
There's more for me,
A cure for my disease,
Ten trillion times tested.

Miraculous Passion

Once a little nobody,
Caring for only oneself,
No intention of good.
Yet now
It's like a miraculous passion
Sprouted far too quickly.
How could you change everything?
Oh, I understand.
You don't really care
About them, or me.
But I won't stop you.
Can't afford to,
Right?
Fascinating, is it not?
It's not.
This sudden change,
This miraculous passion.
I was going to say something,
But I forgot.
I don't care.

People Talking

Look at all these people talking,
Talking about us.
But don't you stress your pretty socks;
I'll sort it out for you.
I can't understand why
These people are talking lies,
But let's show them together.
We'll get the people talking,
Talking about what's so special about us.
We're in it together,
Trust.
Far beyond, we'll go,
Up and up, we go,
We're rising in time,
Rising with rhyme,
Stay seated now, baby.
I'll entertain the audience for you.

Indeed,
People are talking.
We're famous, darling,
Are you proud?
Of course you are.
People talking for us.
Imagine:
You are everyone's talk.

Wow, right?
People talking with us,
Smiles for miles.
Keep dancing to the rhythm of people's talking, baby,
Intricate words leaving the brain,
Then to roll off the slippery tongue;
Like butter it is.
I'm obsessed with you and life,
Like a drug I'm addicted to.
Yeah, baby,
I'm on you.
Keep people talking.

The Kingdom I Love

Tick-tock from the grandfather clock,
Caressing my delicate ears,
Echoing through these walls.
Rubies falling off my chest,
Hit the bare cobblestones, bruised.
Yeah, I can't help but hug the pillars too,
And roll my flat-toned body
Along the sweet, cold walls,
Licking the oldest goblet's golden surface.
I'm sitting on this throne
Throwing sapphires to the ceiling.
Guess I made it
In the kingdom I love.
I took the advice given,
I rose to the top.
Now I have everything I want.
Grown men kissing baby feet,
Grown women serving platinum on emerald platters.
Myself swimming in the ocean of rarities.

The kingdom I love.
I even share the wealth,
Have them stable and in love,
In love with me,
Dressing up each day and night
Like golden syrup.

Paparrazzi all over,
But escapable.
I can spend time alone;
I spend it well
With both adults' work
And child's reward.
Yet I will not be ungrateful.
I will not forget the beautiful people I love.
I will continue to share and entertain.
Indeed, I am not just finished with a single one.
I will use my talent
'Till death do part me from my mortal coil,
Finally recognised genius.
Grateful am I
o the kingdom I love.

Marshmallows

Marshmallows,
Like heaven's pillow of sugary, fatty goodness,
All squishy and colourful.
The true definition of delicious,
So cute and cuddly
You can't help but love them!

Marshmallows,
They're my craze,
Perfect for any occasion.
The way they melt in the already fantastical hot chocolate is magic.
But wait!
No!
The temptation!
It's way too much!

Marshmallows:
The way they stick to you,
It's like they love you.
Perhaps the greatest treat to date.
They're as good as they look!
Marshmealows,
The sweetie for all,
For all a sweetie!

The Final Sentence

You plead for your great cause.
What is so great about this pain?
You answer with calmness and ease.
Admirable, I say.
So this pain,
It leads to a brighter future,
One of peace and love.
And what of your methods to
Attain an impossible world?
Your answer
More empty, hollow,
With a crooked smile and a child's giggle.
These methods,
They go against our rights.
You say that
To create something so perfect,
Somebody has to die?
I suppose
I can't fault your argument.
With suffering comes great gain,
And people like us would know this
All too well …

Our final question to you.
What will be the outcome for us?
Your eyes widen and pupils tighten, gripping my sense of fear.
Your smile literally burns from cheek to cheek,

And then that cutesy tone that couldn't be set on a worse canvas.
But it was the words that pierced me.
What?
You don't mean …?
But you nod,
And so our discussion ends quite quickly upon your proposition.
Listen well, you devil's spawn!
But my confidence begins to die
As I stare deeper into the abyss of no end in your eyes.
I clear my throat.

In conclusion,
We, the court, have decided that you are guilty of multiple disregard for human rights,
For attempted human extinction,
And for the massacre of millions of lives.
This is the final sentence:
We sentence you to death,
Where you will be executed in the most excruciating way.
The date of your demise,
September the sixth.

I held my breath,
What would the response be?
But to my surprise,

It wasn't kicking and screaming,
Or begging.
No,
She had a small smile and deep eyes,
Like she was happy with this result.

I can still remember her words.
'Excruciating?
How unfortunate my fate has become.
I lost,
But it's refreshing to lose,
So I won't be the sore loser.
This is the final sentence, after all.'
Something like that,
Such a unique reaction.
Of course you would remember it word for word.

This would be a statement in our history.
I don't know.
Perhaps they wanted to engrave her mark on the walls of history
Permanently.
But that's a theory I won't spend time on.
This was her final sentence,
The final sentence of our era.

Silent Cry

Friends forever,
Love together.
Freedom for them all;
None could take a fall.
Burning compassion towards each other,
All kind to one another.
No intention to leave one behind;
We are one of a kind.
We feel alive.
No, we will not deprive
Our friends, our friends
Of their golden opportunities.
We shall help them,
Nurture them,
Bring them to their rise.
It's the best thing,
Frightful nights.
We can cover you,
All right.
Aha!
What a bluff, a lie!
Bleeding and sorrow,
Misery pumping through our veins,
Our minds bending,
Breaking.

We betray each other, but we're 'friends',
Lending to the final act
Where you all burn in
Hell!
I see a star and wish
As the beautiful plants
I once held with joy
Became lifeless,
Petals torn apart,
Stems snapped.
We don't seem to realise,
How fragile we really are,
But it's all for oneself here.
Because these roses,
Their thorns latch onto me and drag me,
Along with my silent cry.

Falling

Like an uncontrollable ocean,
Deeper and deeper you go,
Trying to escape,
Losing your breath!
Falling.

Was that the beginning?
The beginning? No.
The end it was,
And a damned one at that.

Yes,
His life was over.
He drowned himself
In the ocean of self-esteem.
He bit into the bait and fell.
Oh, yes, falling.

These jagged mountain edge whisperings fell on someone,
Someone who could fall too.
Dare a crime birthed from a devil spawn speak to me,
So help me, I …

Do you see what you've done?
Do you see him falling?
Of course it hurt him.

It hurt him until he started falling,
Bleeding.
Look at what you've done to that boy!

It dragged him deeper and deeper, the ocean did.
He tried to scream. but no noise could rage from his mouth,
He was thrashing but so immobile.
He was lost in that ocean.

But no one could help him from the height he had fallen.

What them demons have done,
Never show me your parasitic faces again.

Now,
How long ago was it
Since the falling boy
Hit the ground?

Cryin' about It

I seem to see you every day,
And when you see me you say,
'That party was so lit,'
You're actually cryin' about it.
Maybe you drank too much,
And it carried on through your sleep,
But what can I do?
I'm not a doctor who can help you,
Yet you seem to occupy my time.
You're a young, alcoholic fool
Who always seems to drool when I see you,
And upon that fact I turn my nose up.
That's right, I wanna see you,
See you cryin' about it.

No, I'm not the type of guy
Who wishes for others to cry,
But there are always exceptions.
I'm tired of your yapping mouth;
It's drivin' me round the bend,
Nobody wants teardrops
In the fabric of their worn clothes,
Always attention seeking.
Just because you had fun
Doesn't mean you can cry about it.
It's absolute stupidity
For you to think

That anyone would love you,
Anyone would so much as care for you.
You're just a baby.
Leave the man's body be.
We can set you free.
We've been planning,
We've been scheming.
Now I don't see you
Cryin' about it.

I'm Crying

Yes, I'm crying.
Don't judge me.
I make up silly reasons why,
Because I protect you from the truth.
Don't believe it's from a lack of trust.
My standpoint is a view of protection.
I'm crying for reasons deeper and darker than your imagination.
I'm crying over something worth crying for.
Please understand, leave me be.
I'll be there momentarily,
Turn around, be with the group I adore oh so much.
Tomorrow,
A day we can drink together
In an apologetic manner from one to another.
I'm sorry that I'm crying.
Perhaps my cautiousness slipped out of my grasp in an ever-growing comfort to our community,
Dropping and sinking hearts I love dearly over anybody's.
I'm crying again,
But a more longing misery lies down with me as laughs echo through my ears.
Only hatred can be born as clear as my eyes.
Power blows through me
As an unannounced exit occurs in a flash,
Staining my body in blue pride.

I'm crying once more,
I query myself to the endings of my eternal waterfall eyes.
The apartment of smaller stature is secured,
Ready.
In the bathroom I huddle,
A place of madness does it descend to.
Fits of rage staining the walls,
And figurative false evidence lies by me in a compelling manner, of which guilt is placed on the ugly one.
A fatal and final breath escapes my sour blue lungs.
I'm crying contagiously,
But now with the venom of sin,
You're crying.

Meaner

I can't believe it,
That God would bless this world
With someone meaner than itself.
Bliss and plain malice in the pallid face of normality,
Only fitting the description of demonically clever,
Meaner than the ferocious bite of a bullet ant,
More heartbreaking than your last relationship,
Meaner than the enemies of card,
More disturbing than your history.
Your struggle to escape
A futility beyond my comprehension,
As entering your life is a one-way track,
One without your consensual efforts,
Punishment of sin,
God's message of your disgrace.
I'm meaner than your bets.
Counting on luck won't save your sorry soul,
Taking away family, friends,
No means and no ends.
I do what I do
Because I'm meaner,
Meaner than you.

Chapter Two

And we're back.
No fear in my gut as I beat you.
Cross your heart,
Hope you die.
I hear screaming,
When I have the slightest drop of dreaming.
I must be meaner,
Meaner still.
I'm drowning, crowning
Myself, and this abyss is whispering
I must follow it forever.
Together with my beautiful brain,
I'll be meaner,
It gets me so excited, makes my mind go keener.
I swear I'll remain true
To what I need,
So for that I'll stay meaner.
Never bring me down to you.
I will continue to maim you,
To break every inch of your pathetic body.
It's a horrid bubble in my sore mind
To be what they always call the greatest, which is kind,
Praised into senseless, mindless bullying.
I cannot and will not
Let you survive.

Half Complete

There are no consequences,
Merely actions.
That cannot be represented
In the most transparent way.
No matter what was ever tried,
The beast would not be tainted.
This onslaught continued its path of adventure,
Never ending,
A battle of good against evil,
Frightening lives until there is nothing left.
Serpents coiling around innocence,
Crushing, scraping against ill rib cage,
Forcing pitiful lungs to be rid of all oxygen that may have existed,
Turning the eyes bloodshot as the pupils crawl along the white and red landscape.
Desperate for freedom,
The neck clutches onto its last breaths,
And the pale and dry mouth screams,
Screams like there was no tomorrow—
Because there isn't.
And claws dig into his bones,
Tearing this man apart
Like the scraping of a nail on a chalkboard.
But he can keep screaming,
Because nobody will come.

I Can Never Tell

I can never tell,
The time or place.
I can never tell
Between the right or wrong,
I can never tell you secrets,
Can never tell what's going on.
Yes, it is odd,
Watching and staring but not hearing a sound.
Neglect, are you proud?
I can never tell what you are saying.
I can never tell you the joy of running or jumping in the air.
As strange and as odd I may seem,
I can tell you the routines,
The pushing and pulling and stressing and sweating.
I can never tell normal,
But I'm more of the teller of my own kind,
Strange.

Go and Tell Your Friends

It's not a work of art,
Wasn't a piece of cake.
Was it worth it?
Hell, yeah!
It ain't got nothin' on me,
So go,
Go and tell your friends.
They'll just give the same boring chain of reactions.
Our world is ever changing.
Change with it.
It's time for you to grow up,
Done with your stupidity.
So why don't you
Open up that humongous whale mouth of yours
And go and tell your friends?
Trust me,
If you spread the word about how to cure cancer as much as you do with my secrets,
This world would be a peaceful, tranquil place.
So go and tell your friends that,
No?
Sorry, must be hearing things,
Because ain't nobody gonna tell me that you can't fit all them words
In your gluttonous mouth.
I sigh.

Guess you're a lost cause,
Doomed to fail no matter what.
What do I mean?
You never talk facts, always gossip.
When has a true word ever escaped your lungs?
Don't answer that,
Because that would be a lie too.
So go and tell your friends.

Quit acting like you love everybody.
You're a heartless, self-centred coward
With no respect for oneself or his surrounders.
But I don't mind.
Take it like a pinch of salt, right?
Yeah,
Take that salt and rub it into your wounds.
Hurts, don't it?
Whilst you're at it,
Go and tell your friends.
I'm sure they'd love to hear you cry and complain—
Just the usual with an extra side of pain.
'Have a nice day!'
I say.
Knew I'd make you pay.
The regret of inevitability is a simple and stupid feeling.
Go and tell your friends of how puny,
How puny and weak you are.

Your mental fracture of 'me'
Is all you think about.
An ungrateful swine like yourself should wake up and realise,
Have an early morning,
Smell the damn fresh air.
Tell me it's not beautiful.
Perhaps you would speak the truth,
Perhaps not.
Either way,
I'll know the difference,
So go and tell your friends
You still have a chance.
Go ahead—
I want you to.

Count to Three

I'm a single slice of bacon.
Don't need nothin' to complete.
Ain't got time for your games,
No time
To hear your complaints.
Look, this is getting out of hand.
Just leave now;
I need to get ready, I need to please.
If force is necessary,
Then fine by me.
But because I'm nice
And you'll be free,
I'm gonna take my time and patience,
To count to three.

Sugary Sweet

Packed with the calories that I need,
Give me a sugar rush.
I plead,
No need to turn into slush.
You're
Sugary sweet,
We can't deny.
I want to buy;
I won't say bye
To your
Sugary sweet
Personality.
Freedom is upon us;
They will never stop us.
Pull out the puddings and the cakes.
Pull out the ice creams.
Unbox the flakes.
Because
That's just sugary sweet.

Cotton

I have cotton inside of me,
Nowhere to run.
Can't hide at all,
And it's so pure
With flames from tongue surrounding.
Just a singe
Is a lifelong burn,
Indescribable.
The endless fire draws ever closer.
The cotton cannot come back.
A terrible mistake.
I cry and plead for my sake.
The flames just laugh and jeer.
Not only
Do I lose my cotton today,
I lose that one thing
That's so important:
My sanity.

Piece of Cake

I knew from the beginning,
When your party was screaming my name.
I see
What you can be to me.
Freedom—it's not in your grasp.
I can't fall down; it won't be my last.
It's a piece of cake.
I am in control.
The light shines down below, cast before me.
It's a piece of cake.
Wondrous, so wondrous.
Laborious, so laborious.
Filled with hope and cheer,
Frosted with love,
And topped with the power,
Our power,
The world changer's power.
It's a piece of cake.

Sweet, Sweet Heaven

I'll give you that sweet, sweet heaven
When my house comes alive.
Yes, you toyed with me for a little while,
A manipulative, cute little liar.
My heart sank as you sung the words.
No sweet, sweet heaven for you.
It won't be my sweet, sweet heaven.
Golden gears run through my brain,
Telling me you're not worth the fame.
Don't come crawling back now; you had your
Own special chance
When I loved you,
But that'll never come back.
It's your loss anyway.
You're not taking back—
Not ever, no, never ever.
My sweet, oh so sweet, sweet heaven.

Frosting

Frosting around the cake.
The frosting's the best bit;
Without it,
Cake just isn't a cake.
Don't you find yourself examining the cake,
Looking for the best place to start eating?
It's so funny.
Without frosting,
There wouldn't be a second thought as to where you start eating.
But on the same token,
Cake wouldn't be as popular.
Life truly is cruel.
With frosting, there's a problem.
Without frosting, there's a problem.
It's painful.
Don't you wish
Frosting hadn't a flaw?

Take It Back

Take it back.
Screaming and crying,
The bellowing of a dying hound,
Its sound
Like the scraping of a knife on the fragile bone,
Torn heart and shaken muscle.
Be gone, foul beast!

One that devoured all meaning of life in itself,
Uncaring to the others with only cares for it.
Take it back.
Renowned for love and cheer,
A mess before me,
I do indeed pray all day,
Wishing that it would go away.
I find that I will pay; in the presence I feel afraid.
I myself will purge this fright,
For if you can't,
I'll do.

Dressed Up for the Facade

Just pick and choose what you wear,
What you say,
What you hear.
Perfect.
already all dressed up for the facade.
All the fools, they all fall.
Your clothing can be only so good.
The eyes of our soul friends,
They aren't willing to see past the friendly gesture of smiling.
Fools just accept easy is always the best,
But watch them run and decay.
They'll no longer have the chance, the facade a facade.
Nor was it at that, meant to have at all stayed,
Blessing the key to destruction with its locked counterpart.
The introduction and the epilogue to set the undying scene,
Prophesized centuries ago,
An unturning facade
Done for the sake of it.
No longer was it dressed up for the facade.

Cherry Bun

Wow,
It's the cherry bun,
Our childhood dream,
Heavenly delight.
We all rushed towards it,
Not wasting even a second or two.
We couldn't help but push and shove.
It was a normality.
Leave kids to experience something!

The cherry bun was a lesson to me as to anyone else.
There will be someone who's better than us.
That person reaps the words,
But it also taught us that if we want the delights,
To work hard is to gain my fill.
You could've bet a million safely that I did.
In my head, oh, I would get that cherry bun.
That cherry bun gave me determination.
If I don't take what I want, someone else will.

The Muddy Boot

I wait in fear of
The muddy boot.
As the squelching of the soil stained the ever bruised boots,
The banging of the floorboards,
It terrifies me.

The muddy boot
A manifestation of my worst fears.
When he drops them,
It's like the clattering of iron against the floorboards,
Penetrating the body, sending shivers down my spine.

And when, on the days he does return stopping and starting,
Jumping and falling with mellow delight,
Until his bloodshot eyes fall upon me, pray
The muddy boot he does prepare
And turns me around, plain bare.
I shake in fear of those damned shoes,
Not shedding a tear even when bruised.
And so he leers—the muddy boot has been used!

Under the trance and love I am,
The muddy boot will do all harm can.

Big Texas Man

He's a big Texas man.
Everyone knew it as soon as he walked in.
Eight feet tall,
American written all over him.
'Hey there, lil' man.'
He's the big investor.
We dress up, eat big,
Pretend we live his treasure.
Oh, it's a pleasure
To live in leisure,
But just for a day, sir.
When big Texas man visits,
That's what I've heard.
He's a big Texas man,
A mountain of a man,
Charitable church man,
Big puffy cigar,
Rosy cheeks shining in the light.
Looking up at him,
Suit and all, presentable
Forever more.
'How's your day, lil' man?'
Puffing at his cigar,
All the cherries dancing,
I say about my clothes.
He's all chuffed with pride;
I can see it in his eyes.

Took me by surprise,
But it's respect, don't you see?
We all know it couldn't last long.
Lil' man, Lil' man,
What was I to say
About the way we were treated
Every day?
'Is that so, lil' man?'
With a nod and a straight face,
I make sure he's in the right place.
He kept a gaze on me for a while,
The he left. I never knew
What the big Texas man was gonna do.

Just Friends

We're just friends, OK?
I don't trust you enough to stay,
To stay by my side when I cry
About all the bad that happens,
And all the good I have.
I was told to follow my brain and not my heart.
Best piece of advice I could give to you.
We're just friends,
Because I haven't seen the way you treat other.
Just friends,
Because I've seen you run away.
My heart's too big for my body,
Battered too many times;
That's how I learnt.
We're just friends because
It would be a one-way thing.
For now, I'll stay independent,
Independent because
I'm never gonna lie to myself.
I can't betray myself,
I'm never gonna be scared.
Independent because
That's it,
That's all we are.
Just friends.

Poised Abyss

A freak at heart,
With the lowly positivity
Stampeding through your veins.
Deep, deep down,
In the blackness,
The darkest night,
I watch you restless.
Through the smallest corners,
Through the sharpest of edges,
My eyes burn through you.
My glare is an immortal scar into your freak skull.
The poised abyss won't treat you kindly.
You're an outsider,
Not accustomed to our ways,
Our poised abyss—
Not an atmosphere you can enjoy,
An unpleasant surprise for such a young boy.

Darling Angel

You're my darling angel,
Collar round your neck,
Darling angel,
Fetch me my papers.
I need to work.
You're distracting me!
Darling angel,
I want you around me forever.
It fuels me, and I don't want it to go,
But for our future's sakes,
We must only have each other
In thought and memory,
Shared equally
Between two beautiful souls.
Darling angel,
Stay with me now.
After,
Afterwards we can live our dream.
We can stay forever, darling angel.

No Signal

No signal,
No more shaking.
Falling and breaking,
Static fills the air.
What a sound.
Cold, damp, and defeated.
There's no signal left in the air.
Such aggravation the undesirable must feel,
Deceit forced upon the ants.
Though
If you play it solo, then you're bound to rot.
Exploit the queens and kings,
Ruin everything,
And finally
No signal.
Like the ceasing of the wind,
Like a timer running out,
Push and shove and replace.
That's what it means.

Gold Aroma

Awakening my body,
Opening my mind,
That gold aroma.
I can't be blind,
Running on a lush path,
Edging the grass.
It's ready,
Steadily gaining speed.
I find the gold aroma sink in,
A marvellous scent that is inescapable,
Not that I had the desire to do so.
Oh, no.
'Mama!' I do call.
I run to her and jump,
But I jump into nothingness,
Death and decay, overgrowth and despair.
The gold aroma …
It still lingers in the air.

Little Goldilocks

Little Goldilocks
Not the greatest piece of art,
Just part of the big picture.
Burn down the bears' house,
Burn down the town now.
Snatch the kingdom in a snare.
Little Goldilocks—
Such a demon,
Such a sweetheart.
Malice with good intentions,
Wanting of a dark reward.
All the wine cannot be poured.
Scarred faces
For Little Goldilocks' laces.
Knows what's been done,
Finds it rather fun.
Stamp down a little tantrum,
Gets it straight,
No need to blow out the candles.
Let's light them on the cake.

History of the Kids

Beach ball, bench ball,
Play a game with your doll.
Tea party just starting;
Dunk my head in cold water wildly.
Sporty, naughty,
Everything you're wanting.
Put her in a nice dress,
Tell her she's a beautiful lass.
When we've got our history,
Our own mystery,
Something not worth solving,
Video games, for hours so revolting.
Where's the history of the kids?
Place your bids,
Give me an answer.
What's your name?
Play our game,
Dream of fame.
Go out, go out.
That's what we did.
History of the kids,
What's the matter with the trees?
Make a swing from tire and rope.
Let the boys swing vigorously like the captains of the seas.
Let the girls swing elegantly like the goddess they appease.
Climb the rocks, frolic, fields, mountain range, cross-country,
Just in our shorts and our skirts.

We didn't care.
Don't care, don't mind, don't wear
Away,
Like the history,
The history of the kids.

Merry Christmas

The church bell's begun to ring,
And the choir starts to sing.
Oh, what a wonderful thing,
Merry Christmas.
And the decor we do pay.
Please say that Santa will stay.
Oh, what a wonderful day.
And the puddings are all hot;
Mama's cookin' her special pot.
And with the presents, we begin to tie the knots.
Have a Merry Christmas
With all the joy
That shines in your heart.
Thank all for all and have fun
On the happiest of days.
Merry Christmas.

We all rise
To sing our song—
The song of the people,
The song of the road.
Our shining star,
Guide us through our
Fog of sins.
For this,
We sing our song
On this cold December night,

In our church that
Holds us tight.
We all need a little love
On this day.
We move forward from
The barbarism in our way.

And if we love
Like our Father guided,
A new road will illuminate this graceful light.
Let us thank Christ
For this night,
For his sacrifice,
For that strength inside
That burns through.

Merry Christmas.

A Day by the Seaside

A day by the seaside,
Calm and relaxing.
Elaborate sea and mystical sun,
All fears to freedom on the scorching golden sand.
A day in which is indescribable to the taste of an acquired onlooker.
Magical, fancy, and awe; inspiring, precious gems,
One of all kind,
Big or small.
It's a souvenir
Called away to be claimed by the sea,
Ever replacing, repeating.
A smooth breeze dancing with such grace,
Effortlessly like the moving of a feather.
A day by the seaside,
Free and peaceful.

Freak

Nasty little freak.
With your devilish appetite,
Thirst for sadness,
You're never satisfied.
Dirty, filthy freak.
With the face of an angel,
You abuse those wrapped around your finger.
But your shroud of lies don't fool me.
You're sick. I hate to acknowledge your existence.
You're stupid and rely on looks.
You taunt me and tease me,
Just like a Freak.
My life,
Like torture,
But for whatever a reason,
I can't help but fall for you.
It's silly, I know.
I love a freak!

Smarter

I must not deflate;
This intellect in a balloon,
Instead,
Throw the iron barriers.
Allow the undesirable, feeble man
To penetrate such a barrier.
Bludgeoning onto the weak but strong,
Manipulating on the strong but weak,
I'm smarter than when we first met;
I know that you've grown too.
I'm smarter than your teamwork,
I lust for your emotions,
But I can't help that feeling;
It's starting to take over me.
I know the catch.
You're done for, you hear me?

Got older, smarter.
I'm unrecognisable.
Let's play the game I made up when we were kids.
My game,
But I'll play a better strategy.
Watch over, control,
Like camera footage,
I'll play smarter.

Hidden knowledge,
It plays out to code.
Even now, when pen meets paper,
You can't stop the code,
So the one we love oh so much,
Is the one we lose,
Who is both hated and loved,
But only because of the loved mind.
Or perhaps that's predetermined control?
I told you, I'll play it smarter.

I Met You

Everything was fine,
Everyone was fine,
Happy, if you'd prefer.
I was happy.
We all got along
Doing normal activities,
Having fun, socializing,
Sharing common and different ideas.
We had our odd moments, but we were friends.
Events were held and
Memories were made.
I finally had friends to call my own.
They were my friends—
Until we met you.
You took them away,
Away from me!
My friends!

She had them,
Stole them in fact.
Without telling us, she snuck away,
Beating, crying, loathing, breaking.
She broke our hearts one last time.
Just with a quick loop,
My friend stopped forever.

She knew where it was to be done.
She made her excuses.
Heart tampered, too fragile.
Her mind couldn't stop itself.
Like glass, she broke, hitting the ground.
I couldn't even face my friend again.

She was trapped by her own doing;
Betrayal hit her hard.
The swirling vortex enveloped her body.
My friend was charred like my black heart.
None of this ever happened,
Until
I met you,
I hate you.

Watched You Leave

Watched you leave,
On a sour note of utter despair.
Mortify a soul,
Beyond exaggeration and general understanding.
Striking the imposter,
Drowning a pig.
Regret is for the unwilling,
The dross.
I shall not stoop to such levels!
Watched you leave
With your bitterness in heart.
Of course, the inevitable would have us play our cards—
Not together,
This time as opponents.
Our biggest gamble:
Life or death.
Pick and choose.
Of course,
I was the one who watched you leave.

A Million Miles Just to Break a Nose

I could run
A million miles just to break a nose.
Far above in the North of the South,
All the way, the way,
To the deepest lair of the South.
Even when my legs cried, and my cheeks were as red as wine,
When my eyes froze and my fingers were as blue as the sky,
Because I was made in the North,
Raised in the South.
A hybrid respectfully,
With its molten lava
And glacial ice.
Passing by the ugly sights,
Drunkards, loners, little ones,
Passing by.
Finish off a lunch in speed,
Run off in speed,
Impending doom, desirable.
Come for me, you don't.
A million miles just to break a nose.
Thinking of funny
Takes my mind away.
He likes to party,
Chicks around him, loving him, living him,
Every wannabe being him.

Takes me to the day,
Takes me to the day,
Where I break his nose.
Makes him cry and pray,
Because it's not fun
If I have the gun
And I haven't pulled the trigger.

Eleven, Eleven

There was a cold bite of death.
There were babe's tears.
The golden burst of fire on the tired, deceased fields.
The cold trenches thick with mould and decay.
Here, they fought for us.
Here, they died for us.
They who'll glide in the newer peace will never forget.
They who tried, a mere perishing thought of regret.
No peace enlightened upon the scarred and blackened sky could come.
As our country does plea,
Eleven's twice and a dreamed feed.

Eleven, eleven.

I would have had the heavens sacrifice me if I could
For my entire nation,
For my people.
The future tied itself but cut itself to and of these heroes.
Our sun burning away at the thick menace in the sky.
Fight with superior justice.
They begged for their mothers and wives as their bodies were torn from their form as one and so millions gathered in an ocean of frozen mud,
In the selfish pit of hell
Lay the forces of malevolent evil vanquishing our heroes,
The guilt of the eternally blood-stained hands,

The scars and gaping wounds they cried upon.
I remember
Why, the reason, the one reason of these heroes' deaths.
And I thank every last one of you for me,
For us and our stream of alluring hope,
Everything and all of peace,
Company to these, friends.

Eleven, eleven.

And with great virtuousness,
I proudly present my love and forever regard
In an eternally spiralling debt owed to
These heroes who tragedy did befall,
Who fought for me,
For me.
But my world curdles on.
With grave remorse and severe happiness, I'll trial my forever growing memory
For those most definitely beautiful heroes
As I witness your children conceiving the joy of our world.

I pray thanks and kindness to you
For our most relieving and righteous moment,

Eleven, eleven.

Run Away

I give out a sigh.
In the blinking of an eye,
I run across the table side.
With yourself covering my mind,
There's nothing left here to give.
It wouldn't be worth my time to live,
And so I decide I must depart.
Those that are the feeble heart,
I may seem small and frail,
But I'm equally just as tough as every other nail.
The air we breathe, so sweet and pure,
Your magical trait, your difference a cure.
I don't care about what they want;
It's all about making our writing to our font,
I don't care what I have to pay.
Run away.

Mockery

A tragic turncoat.
Of course with malice comes ingenuity,
Impressive without righteousness to one,
Pleasure dug deep in a frail mortal's shell.
Yet with cunning wits,
That weak shelter becomes the great stronghold,
With wise and rational, circular thoughts!
A loop that won't bend,
A ship that won't change its course.
Pounce and leap,
Capture the unsuspecting prey,
A victim of tragedy.
An unkind world spinning away.
What is this?
Mockery?

Gears grinding,
Knives cutting,
Owls hooting.
All's the same,
All is of the norm,
But the one cannot be forgiven,
The one imperfection,
Strangling bloodshot corpses,
Suspended in thin ribbons,
Heavy breathing and bloodied torso.

One cannot merely be forgiven,
Postage of the manuscript pure to advantage's sake,
Foolproof in great believers.
Yet doubt we do succumb to,
No life, no meaning,
Spinning,
And spinning in a dark and lonely hole,
A hole of no ends.
Perhaps the epiphany came afterwards,
But all tasks draped in crimson,
One's mockery.

The Triangle

Peering helplessly
Through tragic, meaningless mist,
Destruction filled our minds.
One goal,
No ends to reaching it.
What no one
Lives like love to play the time,
A darkened project that burns with streams of madness.
To see through one's eyes as perfection,
It's to realise the naive child inside.
I find it broken and corrupt.
To truly gain an honest mentality of such a kind,
One must achieve the impossible.
They would open their third eye,
Embrace that sixth sense,
Embrace it with all their heart and soul.
Immerse yourself, become one
With the last that streaks the blunt heart,
It fails.
Cold and contagious, one loses one's sight.
Musical tunes enter the body and mind.
The clocks grapple your shell.
Freedom is just a petty lie of imagination.
You know,
Control is your passion.
The code source isn't your programmer.

Open your mind,
Reveal your body.
Living for the lust is more full-time
Perfection's will was granted.
Open your third eye.
The triangle has seen it.

Best Last Year

I had so much fun
With you,
With everybody.
That moment,
It'll be buried within me forever.
Our fortunes do greet us with smiles.
I don't care anymore about the past.
I don't.
If you put the pieces into the easiest puzzle places,
You understand!

I'm living, now.
I'm loving in this precise moment.
I don't want this to end, but
I don't want to live in this forever.
My conflictions,
My thoughts,
They don't make sense yet.
I know exactly what I want.

It's not like I forgive them.
How could I?
Even if I wanted to so desperately,
I just want to enjoy the moment.
Let's have the best last year,
OK?

It matters not about the past.
Let's just look to the future—and the food stalls.
Whilst we cannot be with the happiest people,
We can still be the happiest.
So whilst the moment lasts, and the cookies,
Let's have the best last year ever.

I'll Never Forget You

I'll never forget you, OK?
When you leave,
I'm gonna be super sad!
But at least we have each other's numbers!
Of course,
Don't forget to write every once in a while.
We have to keep up the good work we spent time on!

Don't make fun of me, though.
It's only because I care for you,
And that
Is not a laughing matter!
To care for someone
As much as I care for you,
You should treasure it.
I don't mean that in a weird way!
It's just cliché friendship!
I just wanted this to be sweet, so stop laughing at me!
You've just
Always been my best friend.

I'll never forget you.
You'll never forget me.
It doesn't matter what barrier stands in our way.
We're best friends, right?
And our friendship will keep us together!
Maybe one day
We can meet again!

Until then,
You keep working on your writing for me, OK?
I won't stop piano practice either.
When you come back,
We can work on poems together again!
Not only that,
But
I'll play you a fluffy melody
Along with my great performance,

Criminal Brand

I didn't need heroin
To be streetwise.
I am not a gangsta;
Grew up in the house of fallen dancers,
Dancing to the melody of tears crashing.
It's all we have left,
But I don't have to feel sorry.
Dancing thieves,
Can't say I'm that honest.
I don't have three women surrounding me, nearly naked.
Tattoos tell my story.
They don't destroy me.
I didn't need or have the drugs,
Don't own everyone,
Certainly didn't hate everyone.
I grew up kicking balls,
Running millions of miles for fun,
Climbing trees,
Drinking lots of apple juice,
Eating bread.
It was dangerous—
Fires, smoke, and depressing pictures,
Filling my life with cancer and inconsumable cliché candy
without care climbing outside the waves of carcasses,
Cold ice claiming the cream of my colourful car-ride heart,
But pass, and I don't know.

Infatuating my imagination with the mysteries,
Of histories to come.
Yeah, we stayed out late,
Passed a cigarette like babes with lemonade.
It weren't perfect; not everybody is.
Pushed around
With new scenery and the same crowd,
Not knowing my history.
Mother?
What's the word; please tell me.
It was dressing up.
I was fighting hard.
Fight a battle, fight a battle
With rage and fire.
Young 'n' foolish desire.
Hello, big man I admire.
I weren't a friend of a friend,
Helper to the poor,
Healer of the sick
Whose life was spent in good deeds.
I wish I could
Pay God my debts.
All in doing so,
I'll be good to my family,
To my loving wife,
To my beautiful children
Because I don't want them

Being criminals, criminals.
That hellhole didn't treat me right.
I was a wage packet, but now I'm alive.
But I can't take away—
The criminal brand will stay.

This is the life you crave?
I think not.

The Envelope

To hug the envelope so tightly,
Send it off,
Receive it in the post.
Bright letter, bright letter,
Painted blue,
Your favourite colour,
With a little glamour too.
Read this poem,
Just in case it's a letter,
It's a letter,
Just a letter.
An invitation between me and you.

The envelope is fresh in mind.
Cut and trim it down to size.
Sugar-coat these pumpkin pies.
The envelope, the envelope.
Unfold that letter, friend.
See what, dear, I have to send.
Poetry, we know, a whole new trend.
If you have an answer, come on and mend.
I've tried, I've tried, I've tried.

Back at the oak tree,
Sitting near the sunny beach,
What have we here?
Validity and cry, cry.

You got that blue, blue letter
On the sixth, sixth of September.
In the envelope that you still kept,
Read that poem before you slept.
Attention, attention.
Don't go raving on;
We'll sort it out,
Stop the evil wrong.
Deceptive, attentive.
What's so innocent?

The envelope is fresh in mind.
Cut and trim it down to size.
Sugar-coat these pumpkin pies.
It's all OK until one of us dies.
The envelope, the envelope.
Unfold that letter, friend.
See what, dear, I have to send.
Poetry, we know, a whole new trend.
If you have an answer, come on and mend.
I've tried, I've tried, I've tried.

We both know, you and I,
The death was cold to the beholder's eye,
And though we know
They'll never understand,
We'll still walk together,
Hand in hand.

We're darker than the blackest night.
We're never gonna stop, give up a fight.
We're like the cotton candy of kids' dreams,
Or so it seems.
Don't let the sours read the blue letters,
Because it only gets better.
Don't let them blot my poetry
In the deep trees,
In the envelope valley.

New Life

New life
And a spiral cage,
Bending and twisting against reality.
Dark cry calling an ominous abyss,
Crunching reality and throwing it into insanity's imagination.
Let it fiddle with you
Until it's woven something sinful!
Bets and cards,
Winners and losers.
It's your breath of pure air
Before you were to suffocate.
This just wasn't understandable;
Reality was too easy.
We are not what grows beneath us.
Acceptance wasn't an option,
And so
You were created with new life.
The bruising couldn't compare
The hellish desires of this avatar,
The quantity of power it possessed
Beyond a miracle.
At the rate of the undesirable, we stooped,
The victims poised with powerful knowledge,
An ultimate strategy to bury the corpses.
Out and out
A shelter of no safety,

A maze with no ends.
Our own epiphany enslaved the greatest and limpest minds.
The breathing, scraping our lungs,
The lungs, they grow dry.
An opening
Allowing them to shrivel up and die.
There's no stopping it.
Or does hope really exist?

The new life,
A new saviour to this foreign platform of dubious rights and cold ignition.
Our loyalty was plagued by existence,
The, existence.
However, cold burn took away,
Fighting spirit in their stomachs engulfed with despair.
A haunting despair that tore at the flesh of this world,
Struggling, wriggling, oozing, slipping
Into its heart,
Grasping a gentle ball of corrupt kindness.
Can't erase the dead past.
You may be able to fix a broken future
With this new life,
Be a beautiful avatar,
Create a now hopeful world.
A new life without me.

Strange Life

It's strange,
Like an inevitable choice etched into reality,
A torture device only for me,
A torturer myself.
It's some life we live,
Like the script for the ultimate reality TV show.
Of course, it never aired.
Why would it?
Pure torture on an innocent life for no reason.
How sick,
Truly and awfully sick.
I may vomit at this point.
I might just even die.
Is there a point?
You're not a point.
There is no point,
Unless you look at the tip of a blade,
Which reverts back to my previous statement.
It's a strange life, isn't it?

Thorn in My Heart

Today is the day.
I can't hide it no more.
Got a confession to make.
Oh, for my sake,
Please go to them once I'm done.
What did you say?
Excuse me, if you may.
This is what I desired,
Yet I can't stop the pain.
I feel your embrace
Hold me so tightly.
Is this right?
Unstable, poor love.
What can I say?
I dreamed of this moment,
Relived it in my head
Again and again.
This should be the greatest moment in my life.
But I'm sorry, you—
It feels like a thorn in my heart.

I am grateful,
But I cannot understand myself.
Right now
I'm confused.
So just hold me tight,
Don't let go,

Give me your shoulder for me to cry on.
All I need is all you give,
Right?
You promise?
I know it's hard right now
For us,
But if we're here for each other,
There's no need to worry.
I say this with heart, yet
There is still that unnerving uncertainty.
You felt it too:
Something terrible is about to happen.
Strength is being snatched from me.
There's still that thorn in my heart.

Chains of Violence

I'm lost,
Lost in my mean thoughts.
I feel like a prisoner,
Prisoner to my own shelter.
Teachings were simple,
Basic,
Like me.
Don't do this; don't do that.
Act this way; talk like them.
Simple instructions
I simply hate it.
But hesitance,
Unwillingness,
It's weak, pathetic, useless.
And so
Out come the chains of violence.
I scream, I cry.
In my confinement,
Rules were rules.
Break them, and they break you.

Loneliness
In our world,
Nothing to enjoy in the present,
Nothing but pain in the past.
Hope for the future
To keep me alive.

Afraid heart and broken eyes.
I kind of sound like … never mind,
What I say is but gibble-gabble,
Meaningless.
Luck wasn't something to count on.
Bets couldn't save me
From the chains of violence.
I suppress my urges to vomit,
To give up and die,
Because I still hope.
Though
If there really are good people out there,
If it really is as kind as I heard,
Why hasn't my champion come to save me yet?

Caged Feelings

Sought out for so long
A meaningful home of right,
One undisturbed
With goal upon goal as a distraction.
Not to make blame,
But rather
Give thanks.
A merciless grave dragging us deeper and deeper.
The farther we go,
These caged feelings,
Like a burst of energy
Flying through my body,
Living in every word,
I speak in truthful faith,
Love and courage; the blind beggar sees more,
More and more and more.
I want to help you.
It'll settle down all in good time.
These caged feelings can't be ignored.

Feeling the Heat

The Sunday sun teases my skin.
Take me out,
Not worrying at all
About who sees.
It's amazing,
Feeling like a God-given flower
In the power of
Silence, the crows of the fields.
I want a beach,
I want the sand,
Wriggling, wiggling, funny sticking to my toes.
It's tickling, music playing ever so softly into my ears
As the waves silently fill up my beachwear.
Can't hold my breath for so long
Inside the water;
It's pulling me strong.
Move, move—sand's getting in my hair,
Water washing away from me.
One moment I've got the rough sand
Covering the blemishes of my skin,
The next, washing away,
Exploiting my imperfections.
Because the water does not care;
It just loves me so.
I'm feeling the heat as the sun goes down.
Burn me gently
Like I'm pain-free.

You can tell by my teeth,
The smiles wide.
I'm feeling the heat now the sun's gone down.
Feeling the heat going round and round in the darkness,
Swirling on our own,
Seashells caressing our shells of love.
There's an audience of fishes.
I'll give them a show tonight!

My Reputation of Daisies

I can see you dressed up, like the pretty white daisies on the white fields of joy,
The ones to which we gather, frolic by the day and gone with night.
Dancing, skipping on a merry tone along the tall and striking grass,
Our hearts bleeding a bright light as it surges through our energetic bodies.
Your white dress twirling through the unknowns of the forest, of the trees.
Climbing atop with a hearty bellow, a calling, to our acquaintances of the high branches.
Come, enjoy the fun we started, play our game until we stop to home and away.
I fall in love when your sweetness surpasses my expectations of the merry summer's day.
Pulling each other together, when our eyes meet, your kiss a rosy red, it lifts my cheeks.
We embrace each other, reading a ballad, a poem of new
Under the moonlight, under the grand trees that have seen wars before me.
We share a feast, falling asleep. Could the night be so clear?
I'm in love, and the stars are shining down on us, a million counting my love.
I hold you forever yet never; you don't seem to mind.
My reputation of daisies, my reputation of daisies.

Every day, I'm strolling through the most beautiful of fields where the grass is the greenest, greenest for me,
You take a chance, raise your glance, stare through me, with a smile and a wave to the faraway boy,
You care to carry on; one last check and then you're gone. I pull out a pen in hand,
A small pen at that. Comfortable with love, I stand, take the pages from my book, and write my poetry.
I stand near the river of the cleansing, washing away my suffering, washing away the ink that blots my brain, my heart, from doing what my heart desires.
Gently cup my hand and see a reflection—yes, it's me.
My love is like the water: it's fresh and it's free, but it's transparent. Can't you see?
Not a soul in the world could understand what you mean to me, what you and I could be.
We could fight for all our dreams, stay together as it seems, love for us, love for you, love for me,
Never tiring our breath, never regretting what is left, never rejecting a girl so pure, never rejecting her. No, sir. What is love, if it will never be?
Passing you like a game is not what's inside my frame. Future wife, I love thee.
In such a drastic world of change, even I can't understand most of this in its entirety.
But, alas, I do say if I can, if I may, we were born to love, and love is our reality.

I can see you in your dress, white with grace, a daisy in my eye. I could not compare you to any fair lady; they'd never stand a chance. You are beauty, you are power. I love you,

May I chance the proposition of life change?

May I say the special words, kneel down, and open up a box for you to see?

You have a white dress for us to admire. You are my wholehearted desire,

And of our acquaintances of high branch, we discovered alone, but now they set apart, come to us. We've found one heart, put together,

You and I, our love is the cure of all our pain and our grief. Hide away from the sorrow that we learnt and live what we are today.

Up with the priest we stand, say our vows, sing our prayers, kiss each other as we title what we are.

I can see my words never left you; the poetry has kept you entranced. There is love in this pen. Don't look—just feel it then. Our glory is sung to our name.

I have travelled wide and far. My reputation of daisies keeping us together when we can't be with one another.

Write together with our reputation of daisies. Remember how we met as children, love and care, only five, only ten, saving each other on that day.

Together we are here to stay, here to love now. Let us pray.
To good fortune and good health we do sleep. With beauty and courage, we lay together.
Toast to the one thing undeniable, unchangeable, unstoppable. I love you, and you know that.
Bring love and luck to me, to you,
To our reputation of daisies!
To my reputation of daisies.

Bones and Heart

A dark theme,
Ongoing and ever flowing.
A maddening, sickening scheme.
No love,
Not anymore.
Talent wasted,
Fear and dread cannot be misused
But abused.
A new case,
The bones and heart are easily breakable.
But it's the kind of damage,
And the kind of cherishing received, that makes the outcome.
An outcome of light?
Darkness?
It's a matter for luck to decide,
Like a game of life and death.
Who lives?
Who dies?
A repetitive cycle
Until there's nothing there,
Nothing.
Could a fragile babe …?
Handle with intensity
A build-up to the finale,
The battle that ends all.
Who wins?
Who loses?

That's our decision,
Is it not?
But can we be certain
That if one was to succeed
And the other fail,
That both routes
Befall our terrible tragedy?

A Statue

A statue.
There is beauty in that admirable art,
A face of pureness.
Rare gems of life,
Calming surface, and sweet sight.
Burnt gratitude,
Formidable spite
Attained through a statue.
Speaker of judgement,
Bringer of kindness.
Negligence is the common almighty foe.
With light does bring the mighty sway of darkness,
A shadow attained through the statue.
More than just a stand,
A decoration.
Symbolism of justice, triumph, bravery, kindness, worship, leadership.
An acceleration of mind and body.

Pure Pain

There's nothing I cannot miss
No matter my feelings,
No matter if it's real or not.
I would travel a million miles
To touch what isn't really there,
Benefit from something new.
Love can't exist,
Not if it isn't real.
Fame is encouraged,
Yet we already placed our successor
But keep trying.
I can't change this world
But can impact it.
So many hours working hard
To provide for smiles,
Smiles that only exist when they get what they want.
It's pure pain, is it not?

Throw poor Mummy and Daddy.
They've served their purpose,
But I want more.
They cry as they crumble and decay.
Time to sling them into this last hellhole.
Yes,
This will be the hell your spirit boils in.
These liars you raised,
They beat you in the end.
You have one last wish:

'Make sure they feel this.'
Can I
Save myself?
It won't happen to me,
This fake joke you're living in.
This
Sick fantasy,
Is that of a novel's work.
When you hit that realisation,
It's too late.
Pure pain, right?

You whimper and fall
As you draw nearer.
Begging and pleading riot your mouth,
Melting down into insignificance,
A mere thorn of a thought.
Then you remember.
Now you realise,
Regretting it all
As you watch the selfish scumbags
Walk by,
And you see only yourself
Apologizing meaningfully for the first time,
Shedding a tear.
Don't think they deserved it.
Time for you to take their place.
Pure pain for us.

Cherries

Delicious cherries,
Ripe and juicy.
They've fallen away from their cherry friends.
Picking them up, cradling them in our arms.
Big, tough cherries and pretty, fragile cherries.
Nurtured by this great man;
He washes them, all clean and fresh,
Gives them a pretty little bed.
He picks one up and walks away.
The cherry, excited for a special surprise, rolls around on the man's palm,
He strokes the cherry in a very odd fashion,
The cherry's excitement drifted away as the man fiddles with its body.
He promises he'll play nice.
Sweaty beads drip from the cherry as it's fondled.
The man draws his mouth closer to the frightened cherry
With malicious intent,
Biting into the berry and sucking out the juice.
In the end,
The man did.
As more cherries were picked,
More cherries were taken out of their beds,
Never to be seen again.
Because cherries are silent,
Never heard.

Blessed Curse

I'm twelve years old.
All I want is to write
Into the path of people's hearts,
Knowing that I am just the same as you.
I want to write for me and you.
I've danced with too many actors.
I run back to my home,
Embrace the real people I know.
They know about my blessed curse;
They acknowledged it first.
I write with passion pure.
I think I finally found our cure.
Break down my verse.
I was wired with a blessed cure.
Oh, I hate what I've seen,
What I've heard.
But I know,
These are lessons,
Lessons I've learned.
And I can't stand
All these fake people I see,
Thinking that my love and work is free,
Tryin' to take away my fame
Just 'cause you were kicked outta the game,
For months on end you tried.
Bet you can't believe I lied.

Your position of power was great;
Now we have changed fate.
The best guy has come on top.
Bet you wish you didn't drop.
I'm twelve years old.
All I want is to write.
This is my blessed curse.

Oh, Romeo, You're Just so Much Fun

Sing a little song
To my baby, so sweet.
I know what you want, and I'll give it to you right now,
Wondering what I want now,
I know I can get what I want, but,
Baby, all I wanted was you.
Sitting on the hard roof,
Starlight up ahead,
Wishing from the North.
Wish is heading to the South-West,
Baby, I'm alone.
On the table,
We can share the throne,
But it's just like horses and stables.
I don't see you, but I know you're there,
This is the one who loves me more,
Baby, I love you and all that you're for.

Glamour, glitz, and blazing out of sight.
Now, I'll drink ahead,
Forget the phase of loneliness.
You're holding me so gently in your arms.
Starstruck, I am staring at the streetlights,
'Magining the moonlight
With only you.
Oh, Romeo, you're just so much fun.
It's never a thought of being shunned.

I love you, I love you not never.
You saved my life,
And I beg you,
Be my lover forever.
I want you kissing me, caressing me in the dark.
Take me to the moon and the darkest side.
Love me like a rose in full bloom,
Serenading love and protecting you with the thorns.
Oh, Romeo, you're just so much fun.
Darting through my mind like an heir in the woods,
Never took the time to untie myself from you.
Nor would I want to,
Feeling every inch of the charm inside.
Break you down, melt you together,
Create something new, something for my pleasure.
Love you too much, I can't contain what has begun.
Oh, Romeo, you're just so much fun.
We're kissing in the dark.
When I'm all alone, I'm praying for you
To come back and love me,
Hold me,
Like you did in the bar every night.
I love you.
Oh, Romeo, you're just so much fun.
I love you, I love you. Do you love me?

When the Ink Dries Up

When the ink dries up,
Lift the pen, give it a scolding,
Give it a big wave around your head.
Lose your mind
In a wave of insane imagination.
When the ink dries up,
Just dance your heart out.
Remember what you know,
For when you restock,
We can write it down.
All the new worlds we make,
All the new emotions that we can take,
When the ink dries up.

The Garden

Such a beautiful place
Filled with tender care.
Absolutely magical.
My beautiful mother takes me by the hand
And leads me out to the garden,
The garden where all my friends grow.
Mother shows me how to feed my friends,
Giving pretty babies comfortable beds.
I caress my smaller friends and hug the big ones.
My bigger friends give us tasty treats that Mother cooks,
And the small friends make the garden really pretty.
And they help animal friends too, don't forget!
My friends are so helpful and caring
In the garden.

Great Flight

Watching you,
I love you so much.
Watching you leave
With wings stronger than my ideals,
This will be a great flight.
Never-ending support from me.
I love, I love, I love you.
There's no pain in this heart,
For I can feel it in yours.
The great flight is what you want,
So spread those wings and thrive,
Enjoy your new life.
I'll write, of course.
You know me!
Ah, good luck.
Go get them!

Advantage

Took advantage over me.
Now, that was kind of sad,
Glazing me with your sweetness before burning me in the oven.
Shame on me and my heart.
As you lured me
With that charm in your voice and eyes of an angel,
Acting as if you cared,
Just to exploit me in the worst ways.
It explains
Your unnatural acts had to be some façade.
Fun whilst it lasted.
Now you're no fun,
Up to the same tricks,
Always burning my brain
With the same lies.
But like my old man told me,
We can all be nasty.
I had known since day one
Of your malicious intent,
And I had taken advantage of the situation,
Feeding you with fake secrets every day.
I knew you would exploit me anyway.
So when people ask about this gossip, I say
The real secrets, the real truth.

I took advantage over you all
Because I knew you couldn't care less for anybody.
Just had to pull my hair and kick my books.
But now the truth is out,
And there's nothing more you can do.

Iron Clenching

In a black room filled with strange men,
This iron clenching, they locked and threw away the key,
Maybe if I'm good, they'll give me a share.
If I'm bad,
Then a few more cuts will set me straight again.
Maybe an hour or two's worth of nighty-nights.
But then I'm back in the game for you,
Melting metal and engraving it on my back.
I keep on screaming, and they're laughing,
Dealing their money and drinking their juice.
These iron clenchings hold me still.
Whatever does a little girl mean to you?

Insanity

Love can blind us
To believe we can make the impossible possible.
I won't even ask.
Just stop—
You're acting selfish and foolish.
Get your head out of the bucket of fantasy.
And those healthy eyes
See the real-life picture painted for you.
But of course you'd deny.
I guess I can understand.
But then you realise
There's no love for the two.
A match burning out,
Though this match isn't special.
Your anger bursts.
All this conflict started because of you.

I know that so many experience this, so I walk,
Raising awareness
To make sure this plague of sadness at least has a cure we can choose to follow.
Life isn't some fairy tale
We all learn,
But this is for those ignorant,
To this fact.
You don't have all the choices you think you do.
Following the heat is the worst decision.

No matter what your friends say.
Everything around us is to extort us of our wealth,
The wealth of paper,
The wealth of happiness,
No mercy to kindness.
I know; I've learnt.
It really hurts us.
I could go on, but
We all learn.

I'm just that strange survivor.
But you wonder,
Would I be better off dead?
Couldn't know the answer to that question.
After all,
We don't know what's next.
So would it really be right for me to say
Any place is better than here?
We aren't here to theorise.
Truth is
With one extra,
Who cares and loves so much,
Just makes this world one person better.
I love everything that we can try together.
I'm not living in a fantasy.
You're just focusing too much on reality.
It's not insanity,
It's love.

Little Scarlet, Baby Scarlet

Little Scarlet, baby Scarlet,
I am
Living for the forever flower,
Painting it
Time and time again,
Because I just love ruining things.
It's my life, it's my job.
I'm a nuisance like good ol' Uncle Bob!
Little Scarlet, baby Scarlet,
What have we here?
A diamond mould filled with plastic tears.
I don't like what you do, Miss Scarlet,
But I'll admit
You put on one hell of a show for us.

The Last Cookie

Tasty, oh, tasty.
Let me get some of that.
All these guys, they swoon.
I'll take 'em soon.
Once upon a time when I actually cared,
That feeling was shared,
But I grabbed the wrong one,
Ate that fat and sugar, and they gave none.
Oh, well.
Just go one more time,
And there it is:
The last cookie.
Love it to the core,
Nibble on the edges,
Inhale its scent forever.
Love the powerful imperfections,
Feel it crumble around my fingertips.
Roll around my tongue,
Let me chew it all over,
Sweet across my lips.
The taste of a biscuit—
I swear I will miss it,
When the last cookie's gone.

Dew

In the morning sun,
After the heavy downpour of yesterday,
Golden droplets of dew
See the palm of green hands.
These careless hands drop the dew,
Allowing it to separate,
But in mid-air,
As the dew glides gracefully along the air,
With that morning sun caressing its beauty
Before lovingly jumping away,
Like a ceremonial dance,
One only on the unknown occasion.
It makes the morning sun that much more special.
That's why I like it so much.

Too High

I'm desperate for it,
I want it so bad.
But only broken glass strokes the bare flesh of my feet,
It tears into me like it did to my heart,
Rolling around in a blur.
A fat man with three eyes stares at me,
And this handsome young woman walks over
To converse with the man.
I wonder to myself,
How is she not …?
But it fades.
I wake up
To the screaming of a babe in distress.
I run to the noise
But vomit …
A blue colour?
It was tasteless but a distinct blue.
All these little girls laughing
And staring at me, pointing at me.
I run to the babe,
Only to see the three-eyed man
Suckling on the bosom of a faceless leper.
More blue escapes my mouth, but before losing consciousness,
Red starts mixing with blue.
I fall onto glass
And finally wake up.
This is too high for me.

I love everything just the way it is.
Getting rid of all I had created,
But the evidence is already there,
Waiting to be discovered.

The Poor Lads

I know there're fakes and lies
That do not dress in this case,
But giving is the best receiving,
Especially to those poor lads.
Let us pay tribute to the poor lads,
The ones who love us so much that they would die for us.
Give to them
And send this message to all you know,
As I will too.
The poor lads have been here for us
And been through so much already.
Let us give them what they need,
Even if it's the smallest thing.
They will treasure it as it is most precious to them.

The Freezing Clock

It burns into my brain
As the old grandfather clock beats to the rhythm of its oldest time,
Striking ten to seven.
A cold chill resonates from the clock.
My heart tries its best to warm me up,
But I just can't.
I slip and slide along the ice floor,
Desperate to grapple the door handle at the opposite end of the corridor.
Five to seven, the clock read as its gears began to shift, slow. and stop,
The freezing clock opened up to reveal
Nearly frozen insides,
And growing ice speeding along the floor, in the air, and along the walls.
The ice chilled me to the bone,
Latching onto my body as the door's hinges froze in place.
I cried for help,
But all I heard was the laughter I had known so well.
Inside the freezing clock,
At the heart of this grandfather clock,
An icicle grew in its length aimed straight towards my chest.
The laughing turned to crying,
Which I knew as well.
The freezing clock chimed a broken and distorted tune of church bells.

Just then, the frozen spear collided with my warm heart, causing a scream for me,
And no laughing or crying played through the freezing clock,
Not anymore,
As I fade away
Into the nothingness of death.

Beautiful

Played all day,
Your voice is angelic,
Your laugh is so special,
Describing all the colours to me.
Dressing me up,
Telling me all the things I can be,
Intimately passing love through warm embrace.
To feel love,
You don't need to see it,
To feel it,
And you showed me that.
We'd be singing lots of songs,
Together eating the sweetest of delicacies.
You'd write and read poems for me every day,
Take me into a beautiful world
That I can really see.
Hiding from me is that beautiful face
That you always describe to me.

Emma

Emma, so bright and beautiful,
A girl unafraid, unfazed, powerful.
Light paths your way as you
Cry in the night.
Free your mind, be your own saviour,
Love yourself just as much as you'd love us.
Girl, it's OK to be a little selfish;
We can't be the selfless slaves to others' lives.
You taught me that now
I'm so amazing.
We fall down, only to land on a bed of cushions,
Beautiful as they rise up to the sky.
Our arms rise and reach out to grasp it.
Emma, that warm, gracious light is in your hands.
I know music is something that brings you joy in life.
Absolutely, we'd pull through.
Emma, the pain, it strangled me,
But you were there to beat it up.
You are free!
You are alive!
Traverse the mountains of the world.
Live like a queen and feel the force collide!
Listen to the ballads played across time!
Glory, power, to you,
To you.
And when it becomes a little too much,
Emma, you and I, we can sit in a small room
And just play video games.

Explore the garden for a day.
Plant a daisy and watch it grow
Until the month of June.
Dance away,
Call it May,
Be May, Be May.
Emma,
You are powerful!
You're a joy to behold!
Forget your imperfections,
Because they're just who you are.
Don't stop.
A gorgeous youth like you
Illuminates the stars,
Brightens up the sunshine,
Makes me smile.
Emma, it doesn't matter if the world hates,
Because I love you, yes, I do.
Power to your name,
It's growing.
I can see what is now.
Love is our magazine;
Communication is the bullet sensation.
Hit us hard,
Hit us fast; we'll last.
We are the guns, and
The trigger is the L-word,

Emma, you deserve it.
Best of all,
You know what it is:
Love, love.
Emma, it's a grand design that
You inspired, and
It's so splendid, marvellous.
Best friends forever now.
I won't forget what you said.
I don't mind attitude
From you. Naughty? Who?
We all need sometimes.
Emma,
My best friend,
I love you.

Alcohol in the Dead of Night

Dripping down
The sewage pipe,
Where all the contents
Are out of sight.
Daddy, Daddy,
You're not so strong,
Leaving me dead on the floor.
You're so wrong,
Left in life.
Bitter, come over.
The sewage pipe,
It cries in the telephone.
All we receive is just a moan,
And crying through
The dirty, dirty one.
But how do I explain
All the cuts
And the bruises,
All the black
And all the red?
Walking round in the dead of night,
Drinking down a couple shots.
Please now, Daddy, don't cry, don't cry.
Alcohol in the dead of night.
Black belt burns me tight
Around the back.
I cry to you, Daddy.

Alcohol in the dead of night.
Daddy, I'm scared.
Punch me like a body bag,
Break all my pink baby fingers,
Throw up all over me.
Dying so slowly.
Daddy,
Why can't you see
The fear in my eyes?

Daydreaming Love

Perhaps if you paid attention,
Didn't lie about all day,
You would learn
That love is attained through reality.
So when you're daydreaming love,
Replay that thought in your mind.
Focus for now,
Set aside your toys.
I'll help you
Through thick and thin;
I'll be there whenever.
Because reality
Is more fun than daydreaming love.
Because what you daydream
Is standing in front of you
With an outstretched arm,
Waiting just for you.

Run Around

Run around, run around.
Joyous kids with the dirt,
A laughing round.
Little boys and little girls
Hanging out, play about.
Nobody can be excluded here.
In our world,
If we can't make the whole world happy,
Then at least we can be happy in a small group.
Young love sprouts from our roots.
We can stand proud in a family's boots,
Run around like we got nothing to lose,
Flying about around our rooms
Just to go out again too.
Run around like it's the best day of our lives,
Because no matter what we do,
I love the best life that belongs to me.

Story Box

Jumping through the window,
Quiet tiptoes through the house.
You and I walk into the room,
The room where all the magic happens,
All the magic
In the story box.
The story box is red and decorated with blue ribbons.
It's rather large and sits there.
It tells us of a great scientist,
A menacing killer, a mega genius!
The story box just goes on.
It's always that when we're comfy,
The story box starts,
Like a music box being wound up a certain few times
And expressing its song.
Sometimes we're anxious,
Sometimes we're scared,
But most of the time we're totally unprepared!
The story box always fascinates us
With tales of the unimaginable.
It allows our minds to jump out the box and walk through the wall—
The impossible, possible!
So we listened to our story box again,
This time bringing our sword and shield!
Paper and pen, by the way.

We wrote in the detail that the story box described,
Word for word,
Page by page.
We wrote until even we begged ourselves to stop.
It was a mystery everybody else had to solve,
Because only we have the story box.
You have to have the story key.
Enjoy!

Meadow Sleep

Bright lights surround me,
A beautiful night,
An unforgettable night.
The imaged branded in my brain
So that it would be forever standing in my mind.
The rushing water that flew unimaginably high,
Ran so far it ran to the sky,
Illuminating round and round, it goes.
Drunk and depressed skies began to glow.
Grass waves to the right,
Shining in the water's little cute light.
Diamonds impossibly big
Surrounding the giant fountain,
That soaked the greatest tree imaginable.
All around us,
Glowing trees
Emanating a soft light caressing my skin.
I smell the beautiful aroma of honey and taste sweet air—
Nature at its finest.
And I danced upon the finest kingdom.
I was wearing the finest clothes
For the finest moment.

I spared a sneak-glance at the boat that had taken me to the centre of the meadow kingdom.
I slumped my body against the boat, but then
It's meadow sleep for me!

I kicked the boat away.
I watched and devoured all of my sights
Like a sibling with cake.
I then fell backwards.
It was time to have a meadow sleep.

To My Best Friend

To my best friend,
I love you so much.
My tears can listen too,
And they fall,
Falling from the cliff edges of the forsaken eyes,
Damned with the truth.
I fall into the carcass of hatred,
Belittling my current position,
Burning the face of integrity and forcing justice to watch in utter horror,
The disgust visible.
The terror and misery surrounding us.
Come fresh and loved, we descended into insanity,
Murdering our minds' normalities,
Their conceptions.
A democracy was destroyed as peasants filmed our lives,
The burning light radiated in frozen cabbage,
Scarring lavender and stripping the human rights of these people.
Crime is afoot and lurks in the dark.
The mystery is left in the home of meat.
A certain people blame kids,
But they aren't to blame
For loving and caring all in the same.
The conscious is deceived, and we're just fine
Hosting parties and eating each other—
Sublime!

Contradictions in the oven's statements,
Wrong judgement is made fair.
The old stork couldn't care.
Trading love is all we need.
Now they're gone, and I need to feed!

To my best friend,
I was interrupted.
Ha!

Adam

Adam, Adam,
Oh me, oh my.
Where do I start?
Can I even stop?
Raised like a mistreated puppy,
Never understood, felt innocent.
But took all the naughties because you were left with nothing but a
String of hope,
A speck of happiness.
Millions were floating around you.
You stuck with them until they stuck together.
Adam, you were born to be loved.
I'll nurture you.
I don't care about the silly distractions.
They don't affect you;
They hold you, just a portion.
Dig deep, and you'll find something as sweet as brown sugar,
Cinnamon's inside you.
Buckle up because you're on a ride,
We're on a ride.
Oh, Musketeer
Won't stay up early to watch the sun rise.
Let the strings strum as we stare triumphantly
At the sea and the bright blue waves,
Pink sky standing on a mountain's edge,

Feeling free.
I hope you feel free.
Side by side, you and me,
We have the strength to fight for our destiny.
It doesn't matter on an open road;
You're still the best.
Fix up a car, take a call at that trashy motel by the side.
It's just a game life plays,
Beautiful waterfalls but factories filling haze
In the sky, so high.
Adam, we can go anywhere,
Be as crazy as we want.
Because we're free,
Insane as can be,
Firing guns, burning, setting fires—we're going up tonight,
Screaming at the top of our lungs like we owe the gods our blood and our might.
Sleeping in the desert, in a tent,
On rocks and
The grinding sand.
Free, don't you see?
Adam, please don't hurt inside.
They don't matter to your life.
You are special, Adam,
If you didn't know, well, now you know.

You say you are not perfect,
Yet we can live in perfection,
Laugh and cry beautifully in the night,
Care for each other.
The love of friendship will always light the end of the tunnel.
I can't wish I was dead anymore,
When you are here in my life.
Won't beat myself to the rhythm of insults thrown at me,
Because perhaps, maybe God doesn't see you in the way that I do.
Perhaps God thinks you are unworthy of the kingdom of heaven.
But God, our loving father, has taught me to forgive us of sin.
Just know you are perfect in my forgiving eyes, Adam.

The Phone Call

Sitting down on a mid-spring morning,
Sipping on my lemon tea,
Staring out at the stacks of hay,
I fear that I'll lose it all
In the blink of an eye.
If that could happen,
Please tell me
Personally, as I request.
Press on with this work, I say.
Involve oneself in the coppicing of my trees;
Instantaneously we drive hardwood.
Incapable of stopping,
Negligence led to my decay.
No, I never spoke a real world;
Nine times a lie burnt your tongue.
The phone call makes its entrance,
Turning my stomach,
Taking toil upon my tender tears.
Easier said than done,
Enticing me with a one-sided offer.
Evil with a saint's face.
Afterwards we abandon,
Appalled at my actions,
Attending an annual aimless article for absolutely abhorrent apes.

Cold Babe's Day

It was a blue November day.
The babe could not say
What he couldn't choose.
Pushed in a little pram,
Holding on to his sister's hand.
The sun was covered in grey;
No misery for the new life, only fun.
But winter has only just begun!
Let us pray, come, let us pray!
Suddenly his momma stopped
Fiddling with her boring locks.
What, really, was there to lose?
The babe looked through the window there.
He was interested whilst sister couldn't care.
The window was chilling, very cold!
The babe's left mitten had a hole.
Peeking through that hole, his left index finger left to groan.
He did not care for that!
He suddenly screamed as his finger burned!
On that day of November, he had learnt
To never be stupid over bold.

Crinkles

There are crinkles on this paper!
Crinkles make me angry.
Like, seriously,
Can crinkles just die or something?
They are so annoying.
This is meant to be a perfect white sheet of paper!
Perfect!
So there's, like, no room for crinkles
Because they're rude, annoying, and, like, so natural.
Ugh,
Like my acne.
I wish we had paper make-up
So that we could get rid of,
Like,
All the crinkles ever.
Hey, wait a minute.
That's, like, a totally awesome idea.
I'm totally a smacker Einstein!
Posted.

New Clothing

There is new clothing.
It's an option, yes,
But why be new
When you can be you?
Yeah, I know it's weird, but I'm me.
Since when did other people gain the right to dictate my style, of all things?
I'm not for new clothing,
I myself find this new clothing unfitting for me.
They say express yourself,
So I'm merely expressing me.
Sure, not everything new is an absolute waste of time,
But what's considered fashionable for some isn't me at all.
I couldn't possibly hope to express myself wearing that.
Like I always say,
People have a look for them;
They just need to express who they are.
There is no limitation, children.
Nor do you have to be what others want.
No new clothing,
Just you clothing.

Cuddly Teddy-teddy Bear

I'm a cuddly teddy-teddy bear,
With beads as eyes and plastic-cold nose.
I like to play and hug and keep you warm.
I like to say, 'I love you,'
Just to see that cheery smile.
I bought cupcakes
On the date of your birth.
Throw them in your face,
Wipe the cream off the side.
We build a little castle
And binge-watch movies all night.
When you get scared,
I'll cuddle you tight,
Keep you warm and safe.
I'm a cuddly teddy-teddy bear,
And that's what I do,
Because we love you too.

Called in Sick

Called in sick. I'm tired of these games.
I need a suitable replacement.
In the meantime,
I can quietly hide away,
Though I'm a little worried
That someone knows,
And I'll be caught.
I'm losing my patience,
Stuck in here all day.
Searching, but I can't communicate,
Or I'll be caught.
I called in sick for a happier result.
Give me time
Knocking my mind around,
Look for the best job.
I can't seem to find it,
And it keeps creeping through my mind.
I keep calling in sick.
Then the doorbell rings.

Oasis

In molten desert of the east,
An oasis lives in the beast.
It's alive but barely holding on.
It's a struggling heaven that doesn't belong.
In the cruel world, the cruel world of dying flames,
Drink from the fountain of love,
Live in the trees up above,
Pick the fruit of God.
You were blessed
In a mess,
Holding you so tight.
The oasis is beautiful and fragile;
It loves the desert
Even though the desert just taints it.
Love, Love.
The oasis, facing;
The desert, suffocating it.
Dying, taking over its life,
The Oasis's heart's pacing,
The desert craving its
Power, no care about its strife.
The Oasis shelters all it needs to,
Protects us from the desert.
But we let go, journey on.
And the desert will attempt,
Throw its best,
Take us to our death.

That is its desire, for us to fester.
The punisher
Of the oasis,
It doesn't love the oasis.
The oasis protects and befriends;
Its love bends
To the whim of the desert.
The desert with no care,
No care at all,
For the oasis.

The Voice at the End of the Phone

The voice at the end of the phone
Is like an angel,
Distorted at the same time,
Singing in a cold rhyme,
Dancing across the line of the tone.
Can't stop talking through the phone,
Telling me what you're taking up,
What you're paying for.

Scarabs can go screw themselves.
I don't want a pest, no.
I just wanna stand here listening to
The voice at the end of the phone.

Don't care about
The small tress,
The starlight.
Don't care about the
Kindness,
About all the family.

The voice at the end of the phone,
Crying to me my name,
Make me feel like an angel.
What's an angel?
Why should I know?
It's not like I care anyway!

Can't stop jumping through all my words.
Meet up?
Why don't we just talk on the phone?
I don't wanna see your ugly face anyway.
Oh, wait—
My phone!
Its battery just ran away!

Where Did the Light Go?

Where did the light go?
Are we just for show?
Does my misery
Make people happy?
I'm so broken,
I'm scared,
I'm lonely.
Why don't
You just
Come and control me,
Me, me.
Watch out, because here I come now,
Off to the set,
Ready to go live now.
Sing on, sing on,
Friday night.
Losing my mind now,
Heading for the big, bad crown now.
But what about when I was just a baby,
So young and feeling super crazy
Bowed down to the masters of my life.
Break down; it's just another of my strife.
Where did the light go?
Where did the light go?
Candles burn out,
Just like your favourite dream.

Yeah,
But they say, so it would seem,
Every cloud has a silver lining.
Being yourself might not be so frightening.
Embrace who you are,
Because you're a superstar!

Maybe you cannot find the light.
Maybe you've lost all your sight.
But with the love
Of ten million strangers,
You can find
The light!

Changing

There's a softer time
Of changing.
Liar's bullets were
To succeed,
Burning through the babies,
Searing through our lives.
But in this world of changing,
Spinning and turning,
I can make it through.
Keep on changing,
Keep on showing love.
There's a burning desire
To leave and find,
To try once more.
It's changing, changing, changing.

In the Valley of Grace

One hundred years ago,
In the cold, in vain
We fired out to the young and the beautiful.
We were young and beautiful.
We could, smell our rotting friends,
Obsessed with love,
With life.
It can't be living
If we don't feel alive.

One hundred years ago,
We fought knee-deep.
Trenches were dead inside,
Merry men who embraced the flower of grey.
We were the dogs of tyrants.
Tell me, who gained from my misery?
And when you look in my eyes,
I hope you will see me.

I send you this, good friends of Great Britain.
In my limitations for king and for country,
With my friends, we breathe deep,
Eyes closed and sweaty beads rolling across our faces
Like the rolling of our magazines in one's rifle.
Today, yesterday, and tomorrow, I have killed and will kill these men.

But then, on the way,
All of the guns mean nothing.
All of them
Shatter like the gravestones.
But I bow down to fate
As it takes me before the guns die down.
I never had the chance to see those signings, but we will live on.

In the valley of grace,
Poppies covering our bodies,
Pouring out to our hearts.
Today is the day you can think of me.
Today is the day you will (not all) disappoint me.
In the valley of grace,
We dream the most wondrous dreams.

At Dusk

At dusk,
When the storm grows bold
And they fall
Down to the earth,
Blood-stained like the rascals,
They see you falling.
Poke them straight through the heart;
They'll keep on crawling.
Their hearts are ice cold—
No more stalling.

At dusk, at dusk,
When the lights are blue,
Cold is hot and black is white too.
At dusk, at dusk,
When jokes fly
Too high,
I feel like I'm going to die
At dusk, at dusk.

At dusk,
I can smell all the inner fear
Breathing into your small ear.
Never felt too cold in here
At dusk, at dusk.

At the Core

At the core,
I sleep, waiting for another chance
To breathe
In the fresh air,
Feel the fields,
The warm light calling me forever.

At the core,
I dream
Of love and happy ever after,
Eat the bread that is gifted,
And drink the blessed wine.
Tulips cover my sore skin.
The sun is colder
When I'm not happy to dream like that,
Never.

At the core,
I'm never breathing,
Leaning in for a kiss.
Can't be forgiven
Dies down with little care
At the core.

Wait for No One

Playing our games,
Dancing in the nighttime,
In our friends spacious room
Decorated top to bottom.
We're all red-faced,
Can't be forgotten.
Some playing on a console,
Some chatting away,
Some jumping on the bed.
But then there's we three
Sitting on a beanbag,
Reading my pretty book.
Compliments thrown around,
Passed like a sweet dispenser.
Keep on passing, keep on passing away.
Burn away my bad dreams as I hug you and laugh at your terrible jokes,
Make you jump around
As a punishment for your humour.
Take a turn on the game—
How do you play?
Snickering echoes as I lose and stamp in my own fit of frustration,
Throw a book in the favourite's face
Just so you would do the same.
Smell that delicious smell—
Dinner's on its way.

Let's be dressed for now and take this all in slowly,
Compliments thrown around,
Passed like a sweet dispenser.
Keep on passing, keep on passin' away.
Go on discussing over our dinner plates,
Sitting around, laughing to the very beats of our core.
I imagine us how we used to be before
On that boring old schoolyard.
I can't afford to go,
But then I look at the beautiful people I have,
And the million that'll hate me more.
I couldn't care for the million even if I tried,
'Cause I'm just the silly little child who lied.
Don't worry if your poor brain is fried;
You'll be remembered as the child who cried.
Compliments thrown around,
Keep on passing, keep on passing away.
Night then clings to us.
We wait, wait for no one.

Collette

Collette, she's so beautiful.
She stuns the audience with her sweet syrup melody.
Dirty deeds, she's not for it, dining delicious banquets.
Calming, curdling, Collette's creamy cry carrying cold seas.
Collette, she runs so perfectly with her two cute, little blue eyes guiding her passage.
The guys and the girls fall in love with her.
She shows the truth,
And she takes her friends on the most fun rides,
Eats the cotton candy,
Burns the boring old papers.
Everybody loves Collette
Because she's perfect.
You can't pretend.
Collette's beautiful.
She's the absolute.

The Crown

I like to write a lot.
I never wait for a specific time;
Just throw me at a desk,
And I'll write away
Forever—well, until I get called.
With a pen in my right hand
And my story box in my left.
Peeking a little through the box,
A melodious voice sings through the box,
The pretty little box.
As rope comes creeping through the box,
Clasping onto my poor soul
And placing the crown upon my head,
Bestowing love and affection upon my sad heart.
Now I stand on an imaginary throne
With the crown
In my happy, happy hand.

Dirty, Smelly Trash Bag

Have you heard?
There's a totally, dirty, smelly trash bag,
And the smell's, like, so bad.
She's the freakiest freak who ever lived,
And, like, nobody likes her.
I heard she totally never washes,
Never brushes.
She's the nastiest pig ever.
But I know the truth.
I know that she was never given a proper home,
Never shown proper manners,
Never socially active.
People push her about and beat her.
She was the kindest person ever,
But still,
She's a dirty, smelly trash bag!

Jackson

Little Jackson, with a silly smile on your face.
Oh, little Jackson, why are you so bad?
Be a little good boy and sit in the corner.
I don't think it's a good idea to play with a lion;
What if he tears you apart?
But oh, little Jackson, he cannot be,
Cannot be hurt,
Because he's just a baby who can scream,
Can't he? Scream out his darkness and lies.
But, little Jackson, I don't think you know
Our lion friend doesn't wait for your saviours.
Instead,
Our lion friend just tears you up.

World of Fun

When upon a sparkling sea,
Drowning in that old ocean,
I cry.
But you sent devotion,
You gave me a reason to fight.
Tell me how you see,
See another person inside me.
Could it be
You're just a genuine plea?

In our world of fun,
When we sing and dance and laugh all day;
World of fun, where we chose to be happy;
World of fun, I think it's OK to say
We're in the world of fun!

No matter that tainted little bruisin',
We'll never give up and just start losing.
When the song is tune,
You know we're telling the truth.
On a gold sunny beach,
Where we're joyful and free,
Perhaps the menace has left me!

In our world of fun,
When we play a little football but still a lot of games;
World of fun, where we chose to be us;

World of fun, I guess it's good to say
We're in our world of fun!
In our world of fun,
World of fun,
When I was lonesome,
You were there to help me.
Black curtains behind the stage I played,
Hidden within the vaults of lies.
But you found every key,
Took me by the hand,
And pulled me out from my sad sheets.
That's right.

You laid the foundations in the first place.
You made it your job and duty.
You!
You built these walls,
All so that our lives could be better.
I merely placed decorations …
In our world of fun!
In our world of fun,
When we play all day but still find something to do;
World of fun, where we change our fate;
World of fun,
Where I know it would be a truth to say
We're in our world of,
Our world of fun!

Innocent Blood

Perhaps, back when we were young,
We could have done what we could never do.
We had failed with all we could do
Because we're silly youths
Who don't spend any time
Gowin', growin',
Not in mind or body.
We started jumping about,
Losing our grades,
Losing our faith,
'Cause we got that
Innocent, innocent blood.
Oh, innocent,
Innocent blood.

Bittersweet Dreams

Dancing
In a meadow with chocolate daisies and cotton trees,
I allowed my heart to bleed
For you and everyone who 'loved' me,
Crumble.
Sitting on a picnic bench, eating away to my sweet heart,
I followed this typical love story,
Left my heart in the freezing cold.
Flying
Away from this bitter reality, I kept the moulded sugar in my aching heart.
I swallowed down in fear; I knew the truth.
Easy it is to gain my heart, but hard it is for me to let go.
Just bittersweet dreams,
A sour lie with sugar covering it,
Crying out for help. How do we call?
Snapped my heart in two,
Drank down all its juice,
Replacing it with grapefruit.

I'm done chasing these bittersweet dreams,
Done with all these stupid fantasies.
Crime rate in my heart beat all per cent,
There's season to repent.
I'm burning up inside.
I don't think there's any reason to hide.
I'm burning all these memories.

I'm done with all these bittersweet dreams.
I'm sick of your sweet lies.
The fizz of your words rots my tummy to the core.
I couldn't care
About all these boring ol' bittersweet dreams.
Bittersweet.

People in Me

Accusin' me of treachery?
Why, I do declare
You are outta your mind
To accuse such an innocent youth
Of such a nasty affair!

We'd never, ever, ever be capable of that.
We're harmless,
Summer-dazed.
Don'tcha think you're pushing my rights?

Well, out with it, vermin.
Such a vulgarity standing before us
Accusing us?
Of all people, you accuse moi?

Wow, can you imagine?
At such a young age, people came running up to you accusing you of such a crime?
You really must have nothing better to do.
We wouldn't do anything like that;
We aren't capable,
Huh?
You found something that connects us to the crime?

Well, go on.
You may as well.

So you come up to my doorstep and accuse me of that?
Ha!
It's all false!
All of it!
You can prove nothing, you hear me?

Huh? You have proof?
Well, then prove it.
Prove I am guilty!

What the hell?
That's not possible,
That's not proof!
No! No! No! No! No!
Lies! Lies! Lies!
All of this!
I was framed! Now, why can't you see that?

Aha—

Stop your blabbering, you nasty little pig!
May you be hung!
May you burnt at the stake!
To hell with you!
You are absolutely wrong if you'd ever believe I was this villain!
I don't know what this game is where you'd point me a criminal,
But you could not be more sorely mistaken!
I will smite you!

Soak the World

I can't believe
That the world could defeat me.
I could crumble,
I could crawl
Whilst we burn up inside,
Whilst the crowd's alive.
Can I
Soak the world
In that gorgeous feeling,
The feeling of belonging?
There's nothing else like it,
Like that oh, so wonderful feeling,
A feeling
That should soak the world.
No matter what,
This world's happiness must be attained through my
Misery.

I could take
The stabbing and the bludgeoning.
I will stumble;
I can promise you
I will fall
Whilst we're punished,
Whilst you live without worry,
I will
Soak this world

In a gorgeous feeling.
What does belonging mean?
Everything else is so perfect,
Belonging.
Who said we needed to belong?
We should soak the world with us,
Forever.
This world can only be happy sometimes
Through our effort.

Fragile Bitterness

Misunderstood,
He said
With that heartbreaking tone.
Others may have snickered, spread rumours,
But I'd preferably listen,
Listen intensely.
He noticed that.
He gave me a taste of his fragile bitterness.
He was a delicate soul burned by the malice of others.
He loved books.
Imaginative, caring, funny—
He had all these qualities,
All that you'd want a friend to have.
Yet the bullies preach no discrimination,
So I begin to doubt.
Distance myself, but he keeps coming back.
It's pitiful; all I can do is laugh.
He stared at me with a wide-eyed expression that day,
Then never spoke to me.
I never saw him eat,
I never saw him smile,
I never saw him look at anyone.
I probably shouldn't worry.
It's just his fragile bitterness.

A Glorious Army

We've a glorious army
That can't be beaten.
As we are powerful,
Our numbers and tactics excel all others.
We're the battery that never dies.
We're the immortal that pushes all boundaries.
Flesh and blood
Combining with gold and earth.
A glorious army like ours
Should be in the history books!
In the papers!
On the media!
Everywhere!
Because it's my glorious army.

Messed Up

I messed up.
I lost what you needed,
What you needed.
I couldn't tell at the time.
I would guess what the difference was.
I messed up.
I forget the most important thing,
The most important thing to me.
I shan't mention it to the mirror;
I can't take it back.
I messed up.
I praised those liars,
Those liars who ruined our lives.
I'll never forgive myself,
I'll never forget what I've done.
I messed up.

Otto

Otto, dear sir,
I say, you seem a good fellow.
Charming and considerate,
Positively friendly, ol' bean.
You do keep up that dashing smile!
What a 'stache, I do say,
Absolutely smashing!
And oh!
Your voice
A melody like Victoria Falls!
Your sense of style too, dear sir!
Yes, yes,
Enthralling.
You've encapsulated me into practical infatuation!
Dear Otto,
I'd be utmost pleased if you were to accompany me for any meeting of your interest!

The Sparrow

The sparrow stares down at me,
Melancholy eyes and frozen heartbeats.
I stand, breathless,
As you fly over my head.
The beautiful sparrow spreads its wings;
They shine so bright
In the chilly winter sun.
The sparrow flies—
Oh, we've only just begun.

Now I'm waiting in the cold,
Staring at you.
Ice is on my skin, and I've cupped my hands.
I've gone and cupped my hands for you.
Oh, little sparrow,
Won't you come on down?
Come and see little ol' me?

Oh, the sparrow that I see all day,
Flying about as it loses its shine in the winter's sun,
As the winter sun is gone.

Clouds are coming around,
Surrounding our town.
I'm running through the slippery streets,
Flying at full speed,
Trying to catch up
To the special sparrow friend.

And he's
Flying high,
Up into the sky.
Try as I might,
I can't run in the skies.
I've lost all my fights.
I'm crying inside.
I just can't deny,
Oh, the little, my little,
My little sparrow friend's gone.

When I Was Cold

When I was cold,
I hid in my warm blanket,
Hid until it was all gone.
Given all that I needed to defend myself
From
The bitter cold.

When I was cold,
I was never brave.
I didn't try and invent.
I was already closer to the receiver's end.
I couldn't cope,
Needed a guide with me.
Nobody could see
When I was cold.

When I was cold,
I didn't breathe fire through the night.
I wouldn't carry on running
In the rain,
Couldn't face my fears.
Already drunken with tears,
All fuelled with my own sad delights.
I've lost all my will to ever fight.
Come now,
Huddle in together
When it's cold.

Nighttime's Cold Light

I can feel
The warm, blue embrace
Tingling my soft, berry skin.
Nighttime's cold light
Calls my name.
With hazel and lily,
Calm,
Melodious song.
The song
Of this cold light
That wraps around my creamy body,
Tempting my sugar-figure into the moon,
The sun,
And the sky.

Sensations

You're offering up your sensations,
Winning me over, winning me over.
Dip my hands into your sensations,
Chatting and laughing.
Now I'll admit
You were real good,
As smooth as butter,
As rich as my finer tea.
You thought you could play me like a fiddle with your sensations,
But in truth,
I'd tangled your fingers before you could start.
Stolen your sensations,
And you wouldn't even know,
Too distracted by friend or foe.

You offer up sensations whilst you talk to me.
I take and wonder,
What does this give to he?
But I wouldn't mind;
I'd take them quite gladly,
Not think about you.
You can't occupy my mind,
Not now that it's out and you've been denied
Of the sensations that I've been keeping in good time.
You're too willing to share,
But gladly I am prepared.

Your sensations no longer have to be there,
And I know …
I've got my sensations for me,
'Cause I love myself, and that's key.
Your suspicions were
Unhealthy!

I'm Still Alive

Even after all this,
I'm still alive.
Congratulate me—
This is an actual achievement.
If you please,
Now I think what comes next
Is dancing on the spot, sleeping in, watching films, and eating a lot.
Sure, you can say I'm smart,
But at the end of the day, I'm a kid to the core.
Don't expect me to be as serious as you thought.
Yeah, I can talk like an adult and understand you,
But I still wanna have fun.
I want to be able to say I got to do all of this when I was young.
Probably why I'm still alive, to be honest.
But I dunno,
I like that line;
It's funny to me.
Because when you're a kid,
Sound and sight is funny.
So I should loosen up,
Appreciate the little things.
Life is for the taking,
And I'm still alive to take it!

Classic

I find it fantastical
When I'm sitting by a friend who
Brings the fire and the passion.
Blessings are a changing power.
These are classic people
Sitting by an open fire,
Drinking a malt and whiskey.
Read a classic to the gentlemen,
Suits and spyglass.
Have a swig of the good ol' potion.
Set me through,
On a classic journey,
Warming my own heart.
A classic day,
Classic.

White, Blue

White, blue,
Through the window of the old town car.
Sipping on pineapple juice,
I want peace on my ride, so
I stare out the window,
Looking at the,
White, blue.
My fingers tapping on the front seat,
Dress in a mess,
And I'm tired too.
I wonder what it's like to feel the white, blue.
Then I see you,
Could have dropped my carton then and there,
Sure to be gobsmacked.
But when somebody so gorgeous comes along,
You couldn't help but sneak a drool.
Just in the moment,
In the mood,
We fly past.
I wished I was invincible
Because if I were,
I'd jump out the car
And run to you.
But I'm not,
So I'll curse in my head,
Look back
At the white, blue.

If You Were a Rose

Might I say
You look beautiful every day.
You exceed all in the precious factor of my heart.
Say yes, and I'll be happy.
Like a rose,
Your passion a deep red.
We can love and live together,
One and the same, you and I, a power,
A power tearing between the very fabric that holds us in chains.
So you know, I love you;
If you were a rose,
I'd pick you.

Praise Death

Praise death
As a little opening,
Gathering, slathering,
Honey on the dying,
Laying in a grave of salt,
Pouring, wounding,
Fatally fleeting down.
Each meter farther it flies,
Burns and churns all your insides.
A million rats
Laughing, hurting.
Praise death,
Torturing, fortune teller.
Can't stop screaming, falling.
Praise with it or die with it.
Praise death.

Reflect

I can reflect
Like a mirror,
Like a bulb in the starlight,
Colours in the sea of darkness.
I can reflect
Like a mirror,
Broken glass
Falling to the soil.
The soil vibrating, illuminating,
Scoring points to an endless game.
I can reflect.
You can reflect.

Set Fire to My Eyes

I was beat when I was born.
I bought a plague,
And I was cured.
For my heart can't break away,
Stones stuck in my shoes.
I can't believe that I exist
In this world,
In this place.
Pour the gasoline.
Blind me, blind me, blind me.
Set fire to my eyes!
Kill me, beat me down to size!
Praise the Lord!
I'm on fire!
I love you all.
Now it's time to die!
I'm a blotch on a page of poetry,
I'm glitch in the code,
I'm poison to the world.
If I had died,
Perhaps you'd have survived,
But I'm alive.
Tear me apart,
Destroy me,
Kill me, kill me, kill me.
Set fire to my eyes!
Break me, hate me for the rest of your life!

Praise the Lord!
I'm on fire!
I hate you all.
Now it's time to die!

Pirates Are Taking My Treasure

I know pirates are taking my treasure.
In the highest vault, they stand,
Torturing my methods.
Hunt me down for my treasure.
And I can't run, I can't hide.
They will break in like thieves in the night,
Stealing away my life.
I can walk, I can die, I can get up and try.
But I,
I find that I'm losing,
Losing to pirates.
Treasure box, treasure box,
I can't see the day I open you,
Because pirates are in my way.
I fear, you say, I know not of the day
They come.
Well, you say, no wrong.
Thieves, what they are but not one.
Western wilds, they speak foreign to me.
Whisper in my ear after slitting the lamb's throat—that's me.
Pirates are taking my treasure,
And I can only turn cold, pale and stone,
As they laugh away,
Drinking to the treasure
That they stole.

Winter's a Cold Wine

You feel the guitar's strum, vibrating with a unique tone for the time of year.
A fire's burning; the ice's being tamed.
We find a freeze taking over, nerves are bold and cold and striking old, and I could fold. But I'd be sold to simple silence seizing signs of sorrow.
Winter's a cold wine that I pour to merry lips,
Ice blue, wine through, times of the two, marrying our lives, holding our own hands.
Why I can't stand to the cold, breathe the wine, it's winter, it's winter.
Honey and syrup is breathless; I can feel trickling, making its way down the stairs.
No one welcomes the poor and the cold, begging its entry.
We deny winter's a cold wine, drink it down at the feast we own.
I pull away; let us see a routine, rhapsody, and rhythm tonight.
Come and feel the wine separate our goal and mind.
Winter's a cold wine, striking my heart, wrapping me and my eyes, blind.
Animals and beasts, beating boats and cars and diamonds—
They are the fastest, fall and breathe, overseas.
We swing a racket, we fire crackers, we drink away.
The night is cold. Let us return; It's all OK.
Winter's a cold wine, and I don't mind; all is fine
On a winter-born night.

Don't Leave Me

Don't leave me.
I'm just a little boy
In a big world,
Trying to hold on to somebody.
But everybody wants someone else.
Please, darling, don't leave me,
I'm all alone, everybody is so cold;
They don't love me
Like you love me. You stay awake at night for me.
Come stay and want me. I know that they won't miss me.
Night, I fall for you; in the night, there's only us two,
Don't leave me
For someone who doesn't want you,
For someone who will not love you like I do,
Like I do.
Don't say I didn't warn you.
Don't say I never loved, because I love you to the stars and beyond.
I just can't stand being near someone
Who left me.

Yawner

I find you so unpleasant.
I'm a yawner to you, but you don't know why.
You think I'm just tired basically all the time.
Technically, you'd be correct, but there's a contradiction
In what you say and where you play.
You just bore me.
I'm a yawner to you, yet you can't seem to see
When we're not together, I'm wide wake;
I cannot feel the pain of having to listen to you.
I wonder why you act to care
When we all know you're not the fair.
Perhaps you're just too stupid to realise.
If that's the case, I'll make it clear,
I'll make it so for everyone to hear.
I'm not a yawner; can't you see?
It's not what I was meant to be.
I fell from the sky on my knees.
I pray to God, I pray and plea
For the day, that you are gone,
For the day that I belong.
I'm not a yawner; can't you see?
It's just what life has given me.

Xenophobia

Xenophobia
In depth, in the sea.
I want love, I want to be free
From the ones who say they're friends,
Say that they will make amends,
Can't see the light. I see it all.
I burn the light inside, hide the flame, hide my fall.
But all of them, they see it too.
I hide away, but they've found the truth.
Xenophobia, what do you say?
These foreign starters want to play.
What do I say? I'm a broken toy.
They infest inside, creep and crawl around my mind.
Don't say I can't help myself,
For I know I've grown.
I am stronger than these insects creeping into my brain.
What do I say?
Where do I go today?
Xenophobia, don't guide me;
I know the way. I can expel
These inner demons—they can't stay here.
I have the walls, I build them all; this is my mind.
I love you all, Xenophobia. I don't need
You to terrify them, and they don't feed.

Shot Down

Shot down to the beat of the drums.
Why so sudden
With your accusations?
You know I'm just a poor baby,
Don't know how to tie my shoes,
Let alone point a gun.
Can't even speak, but I'm fighting a war.
Don't tell me I can,
When I'm going to die.
Baby eyes won't work.
You're a heartless monster inside.
Shot down without mercy or patience,
No love, no life,
No concept of the human child.
Can't carry on
Whilst I'm bleeding away,
Crawling as far as I can go.
But you will stamp down, gun out ready to fire.
Don't love my dead body; it doesn't deserve that.
Just choke on your gun
And fire a bullet. Could you be so kind?

Shot down like a beautiful stag,
Burned alive just to pour that salt.
Couldn't take a turn for love or my life.
Burn in hell, you demon.

Take some pills;
They'll drop you down to the floor.
Shoot yourself or crackle in the flames.
Drown yourself and starve yourself of me,
Because I know you've got all the desire in the world,
But I can't help but run in the way, oh, no.
Stab away until you reach your heart.
Burn your liver and kidneys, oh,
Shot down like a dirty criminal,
Yet you're the one creating a crime.
I'll pour sugar down your throat,
Stick a lolly in your eye.
Oh dear, oh no.
A billion pounds you tried to shoot down,
But you failed miserably.

For the Love of It

Running off
To the only place where the grass is greener,
Sugar is sweeter,
Diamonds shine brighter than any of your fake smiles,
And I'm the king of the world.
Because pain doesn't exist
In the world of the beautiful.
I'm gonna put that on the table,
Stay inside for a whole week,
Smell the fresh air,
Breathe it in like the pie in the oven.
Pages flying all around the world,
Flying from London to New York City,
And I keep going round and round,
Writing for years
Every day
For the love of it.

Beyond

When I cry about you,
When I cry to myself,
When I'm cold,
When I'm with you,
It makes me feel alive, it makes me feel alive.
But you're beyond my reach.
I preach
To your behaviour;
You're not my saviour.
Beyond, beyond,
Crimes I wish I didn't commit for you;
You were just too cruel.
Push me so far that I scream,
Paint my life like an American dream,
Beyond, beyond.
You are a toxicity
When I breathe in your scent.
It's as sweet as lemon juice,
Got me feeling so cold
'Cause I want you,
I don't want you.
'Cause you're beyond, beyond my reach.
I'm beyond, beyond your reach,
Beyond, beyond you,
Never in your reach,
Never but forever beyond.

Captive

I'm held like a prisoner in your chains.
They hold me tight, leaving me
With cuts on my body.
Can't even stand upright.
And if I don't kiss you,
I'd regret it as you punch me in the cheek,
Scream at me,
Make me feel so dirty, worthless.
Tell me that I'm beautiful,
But you just leave me.
When I'm crying,
When I'm losing my mind,
You don't even seem to know.
Understand how to be kind,
'Cause you've held me captive, captive.
You tell me this is true love,
Cut me up and say I'm stuck up.
Blinded by your cold charm,
I pretend you do no harm.
Please hurt me until I can't remember,
Remember what we used to be now.
Call me your fat cow.
Honey, don't release me.
I want your love,
I want your time,
I want you to smack me harder.
Drink, drink more for my sake.

Do it all until my bones break.
Baby, our rough love is not fake.
Sixteen, grade A, doesn't matter—
I'm your little sweetheart every day.
Driving down the highway,
Out on the open road
Where no one goes.
You force me to lose my clothes,
Cut me so deep if I don't.
But I want your lovin'.
And I know it's sick,
But it's love,
And I'm a captive to what I love.

Nostalgia

I bow down to the Lord
And all my saviours,
Wishing I was there with them
Every step of the way,
Even though I know
There was danger.
Oh, I'd still come out and stand by you.
Oh, baby,
Nostalgia,
I've got, sweet, sweet
Nostalgia.
I'll follow the Son, I'll follow the Son.
I can't believe
That I was maimed
In such a 'free country'
For praying night and day,
For hours upon hours
Without food or sleep.
But I'll continue to love all,
Because I'm a son of the greater and almighty,
And love is what he taught me.
Baby, oh, baby,
It's nostalgia.
I wanna feel the love again,
Nostalgia.

When I'm lost
And you did find me,
I pray to you
To come save me!

Nostalgia, nostalgia,
I dream of the day
I can live with you,
Walk among the greatest with you.
Nostalgia, nostalgia.
I dream.

Stop Looking

I don't find your little games so funny,
Don't think you're what I need.
You can't grasp the concept of love;
Pull me around, think you're so tough.
Truth is, you're round my finger, babe.
I couldn't care for you.
Mean it when I say I love you.
Stop looking
For a girlfriend, 'cause I don't want any of it.
Stop looking, stop looking.
Look, just go and ease your desires in the only way you know how.
Aha,
Don't look like that.
You've got your answer fair and square.
Don't come at me,
Don't be a sappy little sucker.
It explains why you and your friends stick to each other.
Aha,
Stop looking.
You're more desperate than my best friend.
Stop looking, stop looking,
'Cause no girl wants a guy too hungry for love.

Memories Fade

Feeling so gorgeous on a Friday morning,
I feel, I feel
Like a queen, like a king,
Like a grand oak tree,
Sturdy, strong, and beautiful.
However,
I felt so awful on the Monday evening.
I felt, I felt
Like a peasant, like a homeless,
Like a lonely bramble,
Cold, sharp, and ugly.
However,
Memories fade,
Like a book's writing over thousands of years.
Memories fade,
And it's wonderful.

Won't Listen to What I Say

You're willing to take a diamond from me,
Willing to start a fight,
But you won't like the end.
Willing to lie and cheat and just pretend,
Say that this is what I asked for.
No,
What I want is what I demand for.
You give me what I want because it's all thanks to me
That you're here,
But you won't listen to what I say.
Think you can run me
Your own way.
Now, that just won't last very long.
You say, Give it a little more time.
I say, Get over, get over, get over it.
But what won't you do?
Won't listen to what I say.

Inspector Shorten-Housen

Recklessly abandon my cool.
Oh, dear.
Now I have to deal with you,
Inspector Shorten-Housen!
Poke me in the back,
What do you want?
He said, Sweets,
Head on down, head on down.
Act like I have to be a big man.
But I digress.
I love him; he loves me.
There's no point.
We all know it's a fact.
Why can't I see?
Because you got
A pillow in my face,
Distract me from my game.
OK, that's it.
Get you squealing, get you giggling.
All the while I'm tickling you,
Inspector Shorten-House!
Tell me that you love me,
Because I love you,
Plus, we all know you do.
It doesn't matter if we fight
Because in the end, it'll turn out all right!
Inspector Shorten-Housen,

Inspector Shorten-Housen,
I'm gonna say sorry to you now,
Because you deserve it.
Don't you worry;
You're my favourite—
Don't tell the others.
I apologize for all I've done
When you were right
And I was wrong.
You will do very well.
I know, I know,
Because I love you,
Inspector Shorten-Housen.

I Can Feel You on My Chest

We were sitting in a warm room,
Spring day, parents away, just us two.
Buried away my sorrow, for the love belonging to you.
I can feel you on my chest,
Breathing into my bosom, my bosom,
Warm lips edging me. Hold you close.
Set me free.
You push me off; the sofa we did lay.
On my back, on the carpet today.
Kiss my lips, hold me tightly, feel my body.
What love, what design.
Wrap your arms around my head; feel you against me.
I'm so hot, this room's too hot.
Coil your legs around my waist,
Bending over and kissing my neck.
I can feel you on my chest.
It feels so good.
I wonder what you love about me,
But I close my eyes and feel your warm breath
Hanging over me.
I love you.

Loner

I'm a loner, wondering what's in it for me.
What's this world? What's its key?
Can you love like I love?
Can you make it satisfying for me?
But oh, no, you find you can't deny, that you can't fix me.
Loner, taking in what's lost, what I cannot see.
Breathing in the oxygen, a waste of energy.
Guess what I found?
I found a candy cane with my name on it,
Sweet like sugar, and tea with spice on it.
Won't fit long in a crowd before I dissipate in the air, in the ground, in the sea, in the clouds.
I find I'm lonely.
Oh, really?
Nobody cares!
About me, or what I have to say.
So shut your mouth—you don't belong anyway.
Loner, what a loner.
I'm sick and tired of following you, so I won't listen anyway.
I'm a loner with morals, and my morals are telling me to stay away from you.
If I'm a robot, I'll accept as long as I don't have to be you.
What a sad, depressing loner I am.
I am a loner, a loner.

Carbon Dioxide

Fire is burning, releasing, taking; oxygen it's making.
Dust, it's making dust.
I want a trial, test my burn.
Time is a burden, and I am churning up a mix of patience.
Silence is a break, and I can take the pain.
Carbon is falling; awake is a time.
Burning a fire is dilution.
I've been hearing proud, loud, giants.
Ash is migrating and I am falling, but this is a part to free the mind.
Carbon dioxide, killing with might and exhaling from the poorer lives.
I live in a fantasy, a cloud of smoke enveloping me.
I praise with holy, oh yeah.
Wonder where I see my hero.
Carbon dioxide, I see the crimes are fine and I am losing my lungs.
I've been breaking down, firing guns and fitting swords.
I am my hero, carbon, carbon, carbon.
I want to make it so starry, so scary; I am what I see.
Carbon, carbon, carbon, carbon.
Carbon dioxide, carbon is with me.
Carbon dioxide.

Why Do We Go?

Why do we go?
When the sun sets down,
We are passion on the land and in the sea,
With a mighty 'ho' in the name of ideology.
I follow lovingly,
Never stopping, wondering,
Why do we go?
Setting a land and going for the fire, we row
On, on, on.
And I say, 'Watch it, boy. You're only twelve.'
Just getting by, curious as you are, you can't ask why.
Photographs we take on the road we make up,
Designin' what's alive, 'n' I can see you rollin'.
Pass on the venture, won't settle for a few, make half-a-penny.
Then it's all over for you.
Why do we go?
In the deserts, we roam, lost and starved ahead.
But we struggle, believing in our hearts that we won't lose to the power
Of nature, what it brings, what it says, what it means.
One day I struck a feather, and I know it was wrong, but I couldn't control myself.
I couldn't leave him; I couldn't love him at all.
It don't matter what they want to say to me. I'm a good, oh, 'mother'
Take it from me: I don't want any trouble, honey.
Grey as day, but it's plain in every way.

I can't seem to find the Lord who persecutes me, prejudice, all that I see.
Murder is alive, and it's breathing in our fellow-ship,
Why so angry when I fallin', when I droppin',
Talk so hard and melt so fast in a stardust way.
I am falling, falling,
And you're leaving me behind.
Why do we go?

Wandering in the Stars

Wandering around a pool in the sky,
An endless pool with no land.
One second and I'm away, gone, lost
In a valley, in an ocean, of lost memories.
A soul is a soul, and that's what I need.
I'm wandering in the stars,
Wandering along, picking out my part
In a barren landing, facing the world,
Facing power. Love is a crime.
Wandering with my stars.
They're all mine to choose.

White Pony

I want to gallop freely
Like the white pony in the countryside,
Where farmers farm the crops,
The tourists take pictures,
And the white pony awaits its love.
But when the white pony receives none,
It keeps its head up high,
Gallops to the sun and onwards.
I want to shine like the pony,
Its strength, its beauty.
You can't compare to the many;
It masses in itself.
I love, I love, I love.
What's come this far
Is so strong.
White pony, riding in the wind,
Carry me away with your hidden scars.
I'll love you to the God's mountains and the earth's hills.

We Meet a Day

We meet a day
Just to say, What's going on?
How are you doing, pal?
It's been so long,
I am forgetting all the times we spent together.
You and I, loving each other, could never be easier.
I'm wondering what I said to you on that day.
Can't pinpoint it,
But I've got butterflies
In my stomach, in my mind.
I'm clearly red, and I hate it.
We meet a fine summer's day
In the parkland.
Why do we keep seeing each other?
You know, it doesn't matter;
I'm just enjoying my day.
You give me a gift—what a surprise!
On a Saturday a golden chain, my, my.
Wow, oh wow, what can I say?
But then lock your eyes into mine, but for some reason I can't pull away.
Your arms are wrapped around my waist.
You whisper to me,
'Want to know what you couldn't remember saying to me?'
I nod instinctively, a summer's breeze blowing up my hair.
To my surprise you say,
'I love you.'

Just then, I realise why these butterflies are surrounding me.
You push your lips right into mine.
I relax, I take in what's happening.
We meet a day,
And now, I just can't wait.
Jumping on you like a kid,
We end up falling, no surprise.
I have love, I have it all.
But then, and when, we met one day,
You asked me.
Oh, I love you.
You asked me for the answer. Yes.

Can't Ask for Apologies

What is the way of the road to hell?
Is it the one where one can die?
If it is, then hell, just take me in.
Any world is better than mine.
The grass'll never change unless it dies.
The sun'll never go out in front of my eyes.
Bones start to break when the losers take and the winners cry in a corner.
Can't ask, can't ask for apologies.
My course won't change.
Set sail on a rotting ship, hope I drown. If not, the demons of the sea can take me.
Pouring gasoline and lighting a match, and the ocean's set alight.
Oh, imagine that—
Singing in the fire, singing a song as my lungs fill up with broken flames.
Start to cry, like a run-down music box,
Worn out through time.
But I can't ask for apologies.
I'm holding up.
Can't ask for apologies,
So let's watch the fire burn.

My Wednesday

I had a fabulous Wednesday.
Don't ask why; it's just how it is.
Love me for who I am, not for what I want or what I idolize,
Which—oops!—isn't much anyway.
I had a summery Wednesday in the winter,
And it's glowing brighter than the sun,
Glowing for the world and burning in the sky.
On that calendar, it gets a big fat cross from me.
My Wednesday wasn't just a Wednesday;
It was a me day,
A day to remember for a long while.
Wednesday.

Play and See

Play and see
All the wonderful trinkets
That I used to play,
Wonderland's a mess if we don't play and see.
You and me, time's running out—we're gonna be late,
Mad Hatter's gonna stop and say,
'Come on. You were meant to play and see!'
I'll dance to the fireworks that don't exist.
I'll dance in the memory of our lost kids;
They would want to play, play and see.
But the fair few believe they should have suffered and died,
all those thousands.
I've been hearing symphonies.
I can see, the olden way,
Broken and feeling minor today.
I can smell the sweet rose; though cuts exist, we fail to be
What our ancestors dreamed.
Play and see
The game we have to play,
The way we were numbers to them—
A cost to ours and a victory to them.
We were dead, we were dead, we were dead.
We are dying, playing and seeing for the first time.
In 2018, we fell, down six feet under, forgotten and never
brought justice to.

You say it fair to keep those who killed me.
I have played, I have seen.
Those who are here
Must die for me.

Whoops, I Say

Whoops, I say when I don't even feel
The pain you say I'm meant to feel.
When, I can never tell.
Why the pain? Oh dear, oh dear!
Whoops, I say that you decree lies to my sorrow,
Spreading the word that I fall,
Stopping and starting.
Whoops, I say,
I say.
Inform me of my mistakes.
Whoops, I say, I'm lost and I've fallen.

Won a Game

I won a game; frail in the mind, and you lose.
Your anger burns in a youthful flare of naiveté,
Careless, reckless, and buried alive as the core pours out.
A sore soul has won a game
Against a boy; no need to brag, it's just a boy.
Whenever I did gain, I lost and was struck.
I'm not a tamed lion, I won't care for your age,
I'll tear you apart; I am here.
Won a game, won a game,
I … won a game … won a game.
And I play this game. I'm not fair; the rules don't say
Go lenient, do they?
I will win a game, win a game.
I fear I stay easy,
I pour my lungs into the freedom of scenery,
Of a game.
Won a game, and I want to stay, love and live, and burn out,
A candle in the night.
They were fearsome foes,
Dying slowly.
I won a game.

Vermillion

I am a deep shade of darkness.
I know what I have done to deserve this.
Never feeling the blues; orange and red is what I choose.
Vermillion is my name. Don't wear it out.
I have a deep passion for the happiest of arts.
Running from the dark, black and blue,
Running to the yellow, the red, the orange!
I am vermillion; I'm worth all the brownie points you gain.
Let the arts shine through!
Don't deny what must be true.
One more time, I ask in kindness, we do.
Vermillion, vermillion, what's a lie?
What is in it for me, if there's just truth?
There are arts, I can't deny,
But vermllion's my name, and the pretty painting of the sky
Is my art, I am art.

Uncanny

You're so uncanny.
When I met you the very first day,
I knew you were no normal guy.
You started frolicking when I started frightening.
You made the boundaries so unclear.
I have lost my brain in a storm of worship, to the monsters
we call babies and the babies we call monsters.
Uncanny is the term I'd use for you.
Even when you're down and out in the blues,
You can't recover from your trait.
Embrace what you are, not what you are believed to be.
I love you in the sense that
You're not one of them, and you never will be.
God, you're like a dream come true.
I will thank my Lord he sent you down.
Now, to this uncanny business,
I make it appropriate and clear
What it is that we shall fear.
We are heroes.
Oh, yes, we can paralyse
All those under our guise.
An uncanny friend was my hero.

I Am Serene

I make myself a fool.
I paint myself in a luminous green
So that everybody's laughs start seeping.
I woke to fire in my bedroom, I stood alive,
I burned alive.
There's a sweeter side to the rainbow of destruction.
Good luck won't come your way unless you make it happen.
Make the tides turn away to drown the lies draped in faeces.
I fell to the monsters that loved me,
But I know I have the one power, the power that'll set me free.
I am serene, I am the future of what's to come,
And what I see fit takes grace to make it so it existed.
I sold my right to speak for my serenity.
For eternity, I speak in the times of gone.
I live; I don't just exist.
I am serene, I'm the passion of a raging fire.
I'm what stays alive.
I'm what brings you down, I'm what takes you down.
I am serene!
I am serene!
And I was born serene!

Quell

I take upon myself a job which can be carried out only by me.
A toxic, misunderstood face of an undistinct but existing angel.
Quell these feelings as a mixture of love and hate fill my guts.
Repulsory and given rights to remain the same.
I take it a simple mistake, making in the progress an acceptable attitude.
Wonderment isn't to be misinterpreted, false action taken unlightly.
A fist of rage falls upon broken hearts.
Murder is free, timeless, misinterpreted as they say it be.
I see it: a farce, dire and believable, terror inspiring.
Find it in my heart to take what doesn't live, I do not.
It is clear to both us and them: it does not exist in light of love to laughter.
Taken a soul, believe it or not, I had the blow, the chance, the forcing.
It was made, I was made.
Shall we not quell? By what a nature speak this way?
I find a compulsory, targeting simple tears.
I am to quell, destruction, thrashing against the poorer gainers.

Misanthrope

Why are the people of the world so irritating?
Why do they continue in their reign?
Be it nonsensical, be it far from the truth.
Misanthrope, be a word to describe me.
Now leave—I can't be disturbed.
I am alone when I am free.
Taping my mouth shut to stop myself going on,
Signing for the wonderment.
Can we find the worst of the worst?
A misanthrope.
Misanthrope by name, misanthrope by nature.
Mr. Misanthrope is such a horrid man, they say.
I care not for those, I care to only feed on the scavengers that plague this world.
Show the misanthrope what he's missing, if you can do so.

Lucid

I'm like a window, of a house in the North,
I tell you all now I can't hide who I am, but I can hide myself away.
I'm lucid, and I don't mind your labels.
I'm a lucid man without much hope of retrieval through the winds of life.
Not much in it for me; desolate, never free.
I hold myself accountable for the biggest mistake I made.
Made me-self lucid; now I am in the grave.
Lucid, bothering my mind, running round my house in search of answers.
But the waves of stone keep blocking my path,
Keep restricting and breaking me down.
But a lucid man will not die.

Karma

Watch your back, because I'm waiting round the corner.
You beat me down, but now I'm standing taller.
You make a mess;
I do address the situation that's occurring.
You copied me; you lacked in style.
Looked better than me, so you took my aisle.
But you could never have guessed I was coming for a different throne,
Starting a whole war on my own.
You can't stay away when your subjects say, Save us, we pray.
It's never gonna be OK. We're never gonna walk this way again.
I know you're under pressure;
You can feel the power swelling.
Left me to grow.
Whilst you were occupied by pleasing friends,
I've been planning for years, making my whole army's gears work like a charm.
You've been running too long,
You've been making the mess as your kingdom rots.
Karma strikes in the battlefield.
Now I know you've lost your aim,
Got too comfortable, forgot (because you won) that the enemies could play the game.
And I am playing to my advantage.
Just like you, I'll take what I can get.
Never look back, never gonna feel regret.

You cheated your way to the top, and to make you look bad, I'll win by playing a fair game.
You don't decide my fate; if you wanted to, you should have killed me there and then,
On the day you took over.
Karma was watching you since that day.
It brought me a deal I couldn't refuse.
So we went along with this game.
You sat there pigging away, subjects growing unhappy every single. ay,
You took and you took, but you never gave.
I told them all, Don't worry; it's gonna be OK,
I've got a plan, and they all agreed
They could no longer take your greed.
I challenged you, and you made a laugh,
Sat on your horse and charged at me, expecting me to finally fall to the grave.
But we knocked down your men, exterminated your army.
I knocked you down all on my own.
You were the one who finally fell from the throne.
You lay there dying, wondering where you'd gone wrong,
Regretting the past and wanting a future for you.
I gave a quick turn of my sword.
Karma is holding the blade to your heart.
I looked you in the eye, and I smiled with a chuckle.
I pushed down the sword with my very own knuckle.

Your blood poured, and finally I reigned, prepared for the future that someone make me be tame.
But nobody dared challenge the order I made.
Karma, I guess, was the helper, unafraid.
It was all thanks to him, that day and that blade.

Jejune

I fall to the terrible day, Jejune.
I feel, something's out of place, Jejune.
Wonder what I could have made, Jejune.
Would it be OK to say that I don't find this very funny, Jejune?
Wondering why the world only spins on its axis when there's money, Jejune.
How come it's always the same? The poor get poorer and the rich get richer in every single way, Jejune.
But you keep stalling my time, interrupting me with terrible repetition, and a silly and out-of-tune rhythm, Jejune.
You take me, but I already know where I have to go. Don't need a guide; it's not one I despise, not one to take the blame for another, Jejune.
I can feel the end closing near; beggars are the same, just like me. They are wondering when they can be free. Oh, can't we be free of the monsters of the world, Jejune?
Want to play a horrid game, kill them all, and blame it on him? He was an innocent man of the East. He was called a guest to his duplicitous friends; they all gave him the labelling he did not deserve, Jejune.
I'm still wondering what you're doing, why you're saying what you do. Friend or foe—can't tell by your shoes. I'm so lost in this mess of a game that you made to confuse those who play. We are gone because you are here. What's the world if not fear, Jejune?

I think I see now. Pretty lies. You made your mind up; now we're fine. An angel's waiting for us to bring all the things that we can sing in song. Our world is crumbling at your weight. It's time to take down the plate, reveal yourself from your mask. We want you to stop your farce, Jejune.

I am waiting every day for you to come back, and I say you were lost but now you are found. You are shaken but not pale. Can't believe you lied to me, but you were the one who trusted me. Never thought I'd discover your game. I'd unplug it at the end of the day. Will you say what you have done? Of course not, but I don't mind, for can't you see? I'm the one who'll end their misery. Oh dear, Jejune.

Integrity

I have my Integrity, my friends and family.
There's a sweet lie that frightens you, keeps you awake at night.
But, darling, can't you see?
It's all over now; I've already hit the ground.
How dare you, how dare I, strike a fire in the dead of night, praise the Lord for all he's done.
He threw me up; now I'm number one.
Darling, can't you see?
I said it's a sweet lie. Now, count to three.
Be together, love forever and ever.
Integrity guided through my veins like a missile aiming to the sky.
We fly high, we will never lose sight.
Burning in your mind, do not be terrified; we will struggle, but we'll survive.
We will feel alive.
Integrity,
Integrity,
Integrity.
Oh, integrity.
Flames of orange fill our hearts,
Passion burning down these walls
That restricted us.
No longer, no longer, no longer!

I am in integrity.
I found myself in what I did please.
I wrote my heart, I wrote it clear.
I am feeling alive, as is my poetry!

Guise

I face you in a guise, bring it distaste,
But quite simply, in a rosy fashion I make clear an assumption,
Prompt a diagnosis and feel great in wiser words.
I daren't mention the terrors of having to stow past tense in present,
But certain subject matters have to be touched upon.
Yet in my belief, I see it clearer: we take the advantage whilst fresh and strike when the cats are weak.
I put forth this great and simple representation of a plan, in my guise.
Be it bitter, it matters to my preferred tastes and makes it not fair and obvious as to startle our very welcomed yet unwelcomed guests.
I would find it in my heart to place my love in your tender heart, but I see to it that we push forth in desperate times when we remain weak and frail. Be it false, it matters not.
We take what cannot be denied, and we hide them away.
Our agreed plan, is it not?
See?
A guise is useful in plentiful situations, especially when so colourful. You can easily get what you want.

I Say Thank You

Well, hey, I guess it's all thanks to you
That I could succeed my dreams,
Make them a
Reality for me.
When can I
Find the day
Of light? Oh, wait—I know. It's on a Saturday.
But we can make it every day
With my new plan, yeah.
And for that,
I say thank you,
I say thank you
For all my good wealth,
For all my good health.
Oh, bless the Son.
I say thank you.

Take a biscuit,
Because I know you will feed,
And I couldn't be more grateful,
Could I?
I probably can,
But we won't mention
That minor detail.

Cuts and Roses

I don't want to live a life
Inside your walls of cold bitter iron.
I don't want to feel your hands run down me,
Force into my mouth and rub my legs.
Cuts and roses,
Don't want to love
Nor like; don't be
My friend tonight,
For I may just lose my mind.
Cuts and roses,
There's no beauty in what you do.
You don't love,
Only take what Mama stole.
Love what you get,
Not who gives to you.
Cuts and roses, you can't decide.

Hide, what you want, when they're here.
Treat me like a gem.
But we both know it's just a show.
Really, you're a monster
With the face of an angel.
Want to bite me, scratch me, tear me apart.
Honey, I'm scared of you,
But I love you too.
I love you,
Treasure you like a diamond.

But I can't look at you for too long,
Or else I just might die.
You are
The nightmare of my dreams,
My dreams
Just cuts and roses.

But there's someone, there's someone
Who loves me, a friend,
The one with a castle of purity
Who would take me in
And warm me before the fire.
Intruders you'd take down.
The flames that burn will cool my heart,
As there's no more bruising,
No more hurting, no more crying.
Screaming just for a friend,
God heard my plea
And gave life unto me.
Stay. I hold on to your chair so tight.
You promise me that I am safe.

Cuts and roses,
They'll shine through.
A lasting impression on the former child.
There's pureness, kindness,
But your fists up for me?

Not against.
I'll still need time to grow.

No more cuts,
Just beautiful roses.
With power, we'll fall through
Because we're the roses of the future.
Yes, it is,
And we,
Are meant,
To stay.

Centrepiece

You may fall, but I am here
For you and me, the road is clear
To tell me that it's all right.
We both know only with each other,
With our passion, we can make it through.
We are the centrepiece.
Standing tall, we are living our dreams.
We are the centrepiece,
Breathing like we are free.

I may stagger through every mountain.
I may be a stranger to the real world.
But you have shown me what it is to be kind,
And with kindness we will find.
Peace and friendship join our lives.
We are the centrepiece.
Standing tall, we are living our dreams.
We are the centrepiece,
Breathing like we are free.

May our guns fire until the end of time.
We are powerful, and we will love life.
Crimes are not fun, lest they're with you.
Tell a joke, and I'd laugh.
I'd follow it up, and what do you do?
Come, dear friend. Let's enjoy our time.
Forget about the future, forget the real just for a second,

Because we have the centrepiece, and we control our lives.
We are the centrepiece (centrepiece).
Standing tall, we are living our dreams (living our dreams).
We are the centrepiece (centrepiece),
Breathing like we are free (like we are free)!

Peppy Bosom Buddy

Walking in the noon of
Friday, a dream for us.
Meet and chat,
Be fun all day.
Who said 'I don't like it that way'?
You are my
Peppy bosom buddy,
Help me out.
You're ever so lovely.
I can feel freedom,
Taste it like your lollipops.
It's all and all.
Chipper, yes, you and I,
We don't have to say hoorah!
Just snip, snip, snip away!
It doesn't matter if they try to call it professional.
You'll still be my
My peppy bosom buddy!

Gallivanting

Why, I wander in a funny fashion
Like a drunkard taking his passing.
As an open invitation,
I find peace in the merry-go.
Gallivanting away, to a place I will go,
Where my memories will show themselves.
As they climb, they dine, withering, signing.
Gallivanting I go
Across the world.
I'm waiting for a moment where we can go gallivanting.

Fortitude

I found that without a grave, I could fly
When I could have given up.
I could have laid down and died
Against the beating and crashing of the ocean of them.
But I found my own key,
Opened the door, and escaped to take in a breath of the wild.
I'm in fortitude, I made my peace and gave my life.
I never struggled to survive.
Oh, when the wind blows, my dear, I could never hear the burning of their fear.
Fortitude, stay with me; I'm breathing.
Yeah, I know what I need. I'll take what I can get. I'll fight willingly.
My name is in the air; it holds to those it loves so dearly.
But when the storm raged on, I kept my head up strong
And fought against the God of the wind,
Beat him.
I've got strength inside; the gods that pull me down, they cannot deny
I have the power of the gods, yet I'm mortal.
They struggle to push me down. I decimate them all,
Push them down the ground.
No return against my fortitude.
You send your army in just for time to spend,
Yet if you give up, you won't be spared anyway, and so you go on, go on.
Their heads all hung for everyone to see.

I have my fortitude—it is me.
They left no fortitude; their strength was lie of an ego,
And they lost.
They lost!
They lost
To my fortitude,
Belonging to me!

Fervent

I am a fervent. I'm lost and need your arm to hold.
Oh, you love me, you proved your love to me,
And now I want to prove my love to you.
I may not be strong, I may not have the brains of a genius,
but I will defend you no matter what.
Even though he is stronger than you, you are stronger than me, and I have no chance to survive
I'll fight until my bones break.
May my tears strengthen your passion to win, may my blows be a stepping stone for you to finish him.
Fervent, I am bullied day and night, just struggling; loving you's a blessing.
I am afraid, but I will never give up,
I have you to trust, I have you to hold, to love.
My fervent mind is coming together, it's bringing the ice and the fire of passion to melt and burst together!
I'm a fervent, and I am strong, I'm a genius!
And a fervent is not impossible to beat, but I am a challenge!
I have stayed up for nights, stared at the sun, starved myself by feeding off only knowledge.
I'm a fervent, and I am worth more than gold—I am diamond!
And a fervent is not something to mess with, but I am up to the test!

Esoteric

Winning every single game I play,
I know and you don't, you don't believe
In the enlightening one himself,
He gives me my talent; in return, I perform in the highest rank.
Can't lose, won't lose, won't stop today.
I'm never giving up, never going to lose sight of what belongs,
What I see.
Esoteric, you don't understand,
You will never understand.
Esoteric.

My Disposition

I'm a happy, silly guy.
Won't ask you to be polite, even if I tried.
I'm a mess in the morning, for a while at least, because I can't be bothered to sort me-self out.
I'm a little clumsy—make that very clumsy, actually.
You could tell me something's in my way, and I'd walk straight into it!
I wonder about big things in life and keep up my optimism.
My disposition's very laid-back.
I'm no Einstein, but I'm a happy man
With a happy family; my disposition is set.
Cheer on, cheer on, I say!
Drink to my disposition, if you may!

Cynical

I admit to my diagnosis: cynical.
Highly unquestionable, they are nothing but monsters.
I took in a puppy and loved it; it was the best gift.
Then I was with a friend.
Constantly bullied, I was only freed at the end of the day.
One time they came round,
Saw my baby, laughed at me,
Beat me and hurt me.
Holding my baby,
It squealed and it cried.
Perhaps we can see now
They laughed and they laughed and they threw my baby.
They threw him!
They beat him bloody and dying, laying.
He died that day, he died.
I grabbed the weapon that they killed him with.
I attacked them, I attacked them, I attacked them.
They died.
It felt so good to see them in pain;
They were deserving of death.
I'm cynical, and I don't mind.
You call me that when you're not so kind.

Our Love Is Capricious

Our love is capricious.
Baby, don't you know it's true?
I love you for all that you are.
I wonder if you could save my life, when would it be?
I have a stronger ozone layer in my heart
So that we will never melt away.
I'm not afraid to say all will rue the day
When we are split apart;
It would be like an atomic explosion.
We are together always, until death takes its toll.
I couldn't live without you.
Our love is capricious.
It is ever-lasting, never passing, awoken in the day,
Alive completely in the night.
Never giving up on you.
Babe, you're never giving up on me.
We will stay together
Forever.
Our love is capricious, curious.

Benevolent

Why do I fall to the river of the greatest
Benevolent? I know I feel so low.
Behind a tracking in time, I follow down, I follow down.
Start up a perfect engine, a source of light, making sure I do all that I can.
Benevolent signs are soaring to the sky each day.
Minus love, mine is love. I find a path all on my own.
I push through, make it down on my own.
When is it that I'll find a place in the heaven-like land I own?
Benevolent to the way pressing forward,
I show inconsideration to the ones who claim my life.
Pardon me, but I have a voice, and it brings me to the topic I must discuss.
Electricity running through my heart,
Fire burning in my lungs.
Benevolent, I say.
Can't you see? I'm a ghost in the ring,
Fighting against the ones that sing
To my death, my grave, my pain;
The ones that lose their mind when I am here.
I can't stop, if I can breathe.
Benevolent to the explosion, to the end.

I Am Ambiguous

I looked to seek a box for me,
A place where I was normal, a place where I belong.
I found that no matter where I could relate, I was unwelcomed,
Unable to stay for too long.
But so you know, I never gave up,
Didn't just let the waves carry me.
Danced along to the waves farther than the eye can see.
I found I could be more than just a box.
I found I didn't need to be crammed to be free.
Destiny finds me and follows me; I take it by the hand,
Grant it freedom. Oh, see
What we become when we are just free.
I start falling out with the people, start jumping into the world.
I run alongside the animals that chase me off,
Wondering, What it could mean? What I could be
I don't mind when they call me a freak—a compliment shining upon me.
I wait in case of anyone like me; I take them in, love them.
We all deserve love—if not, what is a heart?
I can see in the shadows of the waves.
In my speech, I now know what to say.
I am ambiguous!
I am so much more than this,
A world filled with people.
Well, I'm not a people; I am a person, and I am the one that they will see.

I will never be the last person nor the first, but I can promise you
I exist today, I am merry in my freedom, in myself.
I am ambiguous to the world, to me!
I'm not ready to go in a box.
I'm not ready to be with all the rest.
I love you all, but I just can't resist.
The life that I want, freedom, going round and round.
I'm faster than a cheetah, watching myself rise, and I can't stop, won't stop coming down.
I made myself, and I raised my life to the standard of living, not just existing.
I am ambiguous. I hold my title, I love myself, and I love all of you. What can I say? What can I do?
I know that there are some who'll never get the chance,
Some that'll never see the light. I want to hold them,
I want to know them,
To show us their difference.
You are ambiguous, if you try to be.

Apple-knocker

There's an apple-knocker going round,
Spreading lies around the town, thinking they are telling the truth.
Truth in your mind isn't the same in real life.
Now is it my friend, no.
You are walking around, undignified, no sense of decorum.
Do you find that your opinion is worth more than a dollar?
Unless you be someone worth the time, why should I bother?
Why should you bother?
Apple-knocker, falling on the edge of the road.
And I know you just slipped, but oh, no—
A psycho motorcyclist nearly threw you into the road,
Of course in the most peaceful town in the USA.
We're gonna have a meddling idiot come to play.
We got the guns, we ain't afraid to use 'em.
That's why, my friend, you're the apple-knocker of the town.
Everybody treats you like each other when we're drunk.
But I must tell you there's something else.
You're treated like this all the time.
It's like having a baby who knows how to talk and walk but doesn't know when to stop.
Apple-knocker in the world of make-belief,
If you carry on, you'll die in the middle of your mischief.

Astrobleme

I'll leave my mark on the plates of the earth.
I've got the power to shift them,
I've got the power of a winner.
That's all it takes—the power, the brains.
Astrobleme, I've caught you in my wave of destruction.
Astrobleme, what do you have to say? I'm a miracle of the space,
Of the mysteries that it brings.
I'm all ready for an adventure ahead of me.
I burn hot, but then I cool and reveal my true beauty.
I have a holy dream, and I will make it known to the whole world here.
Astrobleme, it's the turn of the century, oh yeah.
Astrobleme, I'm trying to decide where I go next.

I'm Burning in Barmecide

I took my time to create, I made my own plates
To be worshipped by my brain.
But along came the friendly foe of the West,
And they came and stripped me of my very best.
I can see the light.
I'm burning in Barmecide.
They found me in search of their newer target.
I am lost and alone; they'll take from me what they see fitting.
And I will fire my guns, but to them I am defeated.
Outnumbered to the class, they will shoot the ground. I will taste the ground.
I'm burning in Barmecide.
I couldn't hold back the tears I was using.
I made my walls, I trained my army. I was stamped down in an instant.
And bitter as death may be, I begged for it to never come to me.
But did they care? Would they listen? Not to me, never to me.
I'm feeling their flames and I'm losing my mind, but I am not being beaten just yet.
I'm burning in Barmecide.
A genocide against me, my people, my saviour, my friends, and my family.
I was going to give up; I had died, but I had got up.

I'm wondering what's next in my time. I must hide away, for I will always be defeated.
I'm burning in Barmecide, and I have lost my original goal.
Imaginings are falling from my hands, they are burning from coal into dust.

Uh-oh!

Uh-oh!
The lights fall on us,
Bright lights with power,
Freedom!

Uh-oh!
Uh-oh!
Tell me how we can dance all night.
Tell me now I won't die tonight.
Lights blare in my eyes,
Lights won't break me down to size.
Uh-oh!
Uh-oh!

Uh-oh!
Looks as if I'm gone,
Just a crying mess in my place.
Stealing tomorrow just for this night!

Uh-oh!
Uh-oh!
Winners rise and live a life.
A loser hides to drown in strife.
A loser is what we're meant to be.
Winners are the only ones who are free!
Uh-oh!
Uh-oh!

Uh-oh!
Uh-oh!
Uh-oh!
I'm lost, but that doesn't mean you have to be!
Uh-oh!
Uh-oh!
Uh-oh …

Couthy

Feel so good inside, Couthy.
Losing to the love, when are we going?
I don't leave, I just sleep.
Couthy makes me feel so good, so happy.
I know I can be warmed up any day,
Especially in the winter, hey.
Couthy, let me in, hold me so close; I can never feel
Like I do when I have
Couthy. Couthy, let me in,
I want to live here, right here, Couthy.

I Am That One That'll Degust

Do you know that one friend?
That one friend who just tickles your side bones but annoys you at the same time come mealtime?
I am that one friend,
I am that one that'll degust.
I find it most pleasurable, and whilst you enjoy watching me for a while,
You then get bored, try and hurry me.
But you already know it's never gonna happen,
So I smile smugly and go even slower.
You give the most exaggerated sigh ever and head to the kitchen.
I am that one that'll degust!
But what's this?
You come back with culinary devices and start eating with me?
I can't help but stare.
I don't know whether to laugh or smack you square in the face.
But you look into my eyes, and so I start eating with you.
We're just best friends, so I shouldn't be surprised.
I give a cute, warm smile, and we eat together.
We are the ones that'll degust together.

Imaginings

Imagining, imaginings,
Can there be such cruelty in my mind?
The dolls I play with
Only exist in this world.
But come what may,
We will find our escape
Into the light of imaginings.
Why is it that I lose what belongs to me?
Can't get it back,
Yet I shall try,
Because I am the one who loves his mind.
Ah, freedom, freedom
In the places that I go.
Crimes are not what they seem,
But, oh, you all know
There's still pain in my mind.
I'm imagining
The happiness they bring.
Somehow, I can still feel the burning.
It's not a lie
Just because I dream it all the time.
I'm just an author, a poet
With a dream.
These are stories of fiction,
My own world,
Of imaginings.

Yes, the world (I adore),
Love and peace (conquers my heart),
Here, there's still pain,
But that's just part of our world.
For I have just begun
To tell you of my world,
My imaginings,
An inferno of never-ending dreams.
Gifted with a whisper of my imaginings.
The past is gone,
And we are stronger now.
Living for the life I lead,
A dream of dreams,
Imagine that you lose your mind.
Instead of going insane,
You would just expand your mind.
And even if it means I'm crazy,
At least I know that I'm the best crazy alive.
Be proud of what your mind makes you.
I practically live with mine.
I am a normal child
With abnormal imaginings.

You Are a Baby

We stare at the end
For those who lie.
Six feet under, a patience inside.
Yeah, now you can see the love,
The love of the passed,
The love of me,
The love of your family.
We believe and share your tragedies.
You are a baby,
And I bet she loves you so very much,
Looks down on you,
Cries for you too
Because she had wishes,
Hopes that can't be fulfilled.
We, however, can live our lives.
Still so young, so bright.
Life and future does await
For us, for me, for you.
The sportsman, a talented player.
The writer, the turn of literature.
We can look at the past,
Make our lives last,
Carry on.
But we'll pray
Every night
To those whom we lost.
I send my life to you,

And she surely will too.
You are a baby,
A baby,
You are a baby,
A baby.
Support each other through,
Thick and thin.
We are loved, we are wanted,
And they are loved.
Though they are gone,
That doesn't mean
We should forget.
You and I,
You,
Yes, you,
You are just a beautiful baby,
A baby,
Just a beautiful baby,
A baby.
You are a baby,
Baby.
We are babies,
Just new, not old. We shouldn't have died.
We are babies.

I can still remember
The day her eyes closed.

It sent my body through a fit of despairing spasms
As she took her last breath.
The life in the room dies
Every time I try and
Talk about it.
But at least I know somebody can understand
Why she made me smile,
And why I can't sleep
Knowing she's not here anymore.

You are just a baby,
One with a beautiful heart,
One that cannot be replaced.
We are babies,
Babies.

One moment and the next,
Gone.
Your breath catching along the peaceful November wind.
Your skin a pallid sheet of folding beauty, peaceful, but ice against delicate skin.
I yearn for the blue in your eyes
Because I finally see how much power you truly gave me.
And I have one last message to you, one you'll never hear:
I love you.

I am a baby,
You are a baby.

Dumbsize Goes On

Working through the games I play in time,
Dumbsize goes on.
Cooperating an issue as we find no one can.
We daren't complain as to be founded guilty of some excuse or another.
Dumbsize goes on.
Finding ourselves strapped to a ride,
A ride that can't fit us.
Our job made hell,
A pay packet, mere flimsy paper.
Dumbsize goes on.
Take in chocolate hearts and leave with dissatisfied grunts.
Many are to blame the staff quite quickly.
Whilst the other is getting rich, we are losing it,
But we have no place to go,
Not with our reputation.
We wouldn't be taken on to stack shelves.
We wouldn't be hired if others were desperate.
They'd preferably go out of business than allow us to join their ranks.
Dumbsize goes on.

I Feel Dwaal

My eyes are a canvas, ready to be coloured in by the greatest.
There are colours that suit me, and the ones that can mix to match.
I feel dwaal, I feel dwaal.
Taking a trip down the most memorable places in my world,
I feel dwaal, I feel dwaal.
Silence is a lame, old game. Make more noise than the world.
Shut your eyes and listen to the ones who perform for love,
Perform for life,
Perform for all that the world can bring.
I feel dwaal, I feel dwaal.
Memories, paint the green seas.
Ideas, paint the pink sky.
And the future paints the setting, brown sun of the sky.

Erubescent

I see you on the edge of a mountain,
I call your name.
You turn and give a smile, you hug me and hold me.
As the sun goes down,
You can see I'm clearly Erubescent.
I hate and I love it at the same time.
You're so sweet when you ask if I'm all right,
If I'm all right.
I love it when we play the game, on top of the scary edge.
No fear, no worry in your eyes,
In your eyes.
Erubescent, I dunno how, but I can tell it's in your eyes,
In your eyes.
You say you love my pretty blue dress,
The way it shines like the ocean's water crest.
I smile; erubescent is clear by my side.
But then all of a sudden,
A sudden,
My dress turns erubescent itself now,
It shines a bright crimson in the ultimate sun.
You give me a sweet smile again,
You lift my head up to reveal I'm all erubescent,
Just for you.
You laugh a little yourself,
Open up your arms.

I see your heart is erubescent!
I hug you so tightly, and you hug me back.
Embracing each other on the mountain,
An erubescent mountain,
Mountain.

We Can All Taste the Eye Candy

On the television screen, we don't demand too much.
We only see what it gives to us,
And are pleased enough.
I guess I don't need to stretch my imaginings too far.
I've got eye candy to feed me.
We can all taste the eye candy,
And it's delicious.
But I never needed to work to even taste this.
I hurt the poor blind man by taking his eye candy.
He takes me, he grabs, he holds me, he begs for mercy.
I just kick him away.
Why do I need to work so hard to imagine,
When we can all taste the eye candy?

Many of us Just Futz

Many of us just futz around all day. Oh, it's our break,
So we'll waste all our time, act like a lollygag.
It's not a bad thing, we say, even though our lives just waste away.
Doing nothing but sitting in and eating and eating away.
That's not living.
Many of us just futz, and I can see what terror we cause.
We turn more into skeletons every day.
Even though we get larger,
We get closer to the grave.
We lose what our parents gave.
When we were young, we were more brave.
Now we've just turned into zombie slaves,
Many of us just futz.

Many a Man a Hinky

I say, you hinky of a man,
It's a sorry time for us.
Drink away the pain. I drink too much, and I still remember.
Many a man a hinky, once upon a day.
He makes it to work,
He gets his own way.
I was fired 'cause of a bitter hinky.
If I see one more of those blasted wretches, then throw me in the cell,
'Cause I'll gladly stamp all over his face.
Now, in my world it's very different, you see.
I dunno what you get if you're experiencing something like me
In your hometown; if not, then send them the warmest regards from me.
But in my home, I can't escape all these wretches,
All these horrors of a kind.
Many a man a hinky,
And that don't include me.

Meacock

Meacock, a friendly boy he was, but he was constantly a nuisance at the same time.
He made an embarrassment to his brother, always overlooked under that shadow.
He was calm, kind, and quirky, not much going for him.
He found a lot of trouble everywhere.
Meacock, my word, surprises are met around every corner.
You took on the toughest guy and won?
Impressive; it was the talk of the town.
Though it started up some menacing rivalries,
And that's when you stopped, you left Meacock behind,
And became you without Meacock there.

Could You Really Be Minacious?

Could you really be minacious?
I never saw it myself.
Then again, you never do see it in people like you.
It's always unbelievable no matter how believable it is to some people in the first place.
You just seemed so unfiltered,
Raw, with passion rocking your veins.
You fought for us, you had real arguments. How could you turn to be this?
It's not possible, but it is, but it isn't!
Could you really be minacious?
After our entire adventure, after all that bonding, growing together and fighting for each other, this is what it has come to.
Our entire town devastated. But worse, believing I was part of your horrendous plan and forcing me to become outcast to the town, homeless.
How could you?
Could you really be minacious?
Just let me wake up from this dream.
Why aren't I waking up?

I'm Starting to Feel like a Mouse Potato

I've been typing for so long, got a job; I work at home.
Eat, type, sleep, repeat.
Oh, wow—
I'm starting to feel like a mouse potato,
And you can trust in me that:, that is not a good thing.
My eyes will sag, my bones will numb, my lips go dry, and my fingers run sore for ages, I tell you.
Man, I can't wait to get done with work.
You know how pleased I'd actually be to greet the winter air rather than stay here all day.
Honestly, I'm starting to feel like a mouse potato.
I've never felt more overworked and underworked in my life.
You could get me to chop wood in the freezing cold straight after this, and you shouldn't be surprised if you hear me running through the door, grabbing my clothes, and off I go to do the task set.
My relief when this is done—gosh,
Do I sleep or do I set myself a task?
I honestly don't know,
But I say it'd be fun either way.

Momism

I love my mum so much, I wouldn't trade her for the world.
I love my mum so much that when we joke, I make sure she laughs.
It's the most fun of operations. I go through the ranks of hilarity,
But usually she'd quit her seriousness as soon as I can make her belly ache.
I'm proud if you want to say, I've got Momism,
Because I love her so much, Momism.
In my eyes, she lives her dream.
Only we can understand each other.
I'd say we've all got Momism.
All the family,
My mum's the best, and my dad can agree with that.

Star Colours

You want to be a superstar.
You want the fame to come to you.
You want a life of star colours.
You want to say what comes and goes.
Star colours floating in the sky
Above you, above you.
You can barely even see them,
Let alone try and reach them.
Star colours, I can see them in your eyes,
Shining brighter a colour than any.
Living for that golden style,
Faraway, but perhaps, oh,
Perhaps there is a way
To reach what you've been searching for.
Star colours, they're burning brighter than ever before.
They're gonna shine in your hand,
Blow up in sparks as the hero arrives
For the admirers, the dreamers,
The children, the seekers.
All of them will come alive, and you will live your dream for life. Just say to them what is true.
Stand alive—the clock ticks faster, lasts more than a night.
Come and invite your happiness to dine.
Star colours, they're only that because of you.

Why I Be Noyade

Why I be noyade.
To the foundations in support and of care, I say you're not good enough.
Never would it be insulting—rather, final criticism worthy.
Starting to painfully process my indulgence.
I leave
In the easiest way I know how.
Noyade.
The perfect excuse easily made plausible.
Why I be Noyade.
I see it as only a certain but lengthy amount of time before death greets my door unannounced.
I'd preferably meet and dine with death before I be noyade.
Why I be Noyade.
There isn't an excuse of proper reasoning, however I can say
This world is undeserving of myself, and I leave in search of something better.

Peterman to My Love

You came like a thief in the night.
You made your way into my life.
Peterman to my love,
I say you've made yourself a deal in mind.
You'll tell it to me. Won't you be so kind?
I grew to love you. You have my heart cupped in your hand, but what else?
You give my heart back to me and open your hands, opening a case.
You reveal to me a glowing diamond. You stare into my eyes and say those magical words.
I say, Yes!
Can you believe our love brought us together?
Thievery can make something beautiful—at least, that's what our story has done for us.
Peterman to my love,
Steal away my heart and be my lover.

Pre-loved Friend

I hold you dear to my heart, at least when you weren't
A pre-loved friend.
I hold the memories, the best ones and the bad,
But I hate you more than ever now.
You're just second-hand,
A pre-loved friend.
You're not a man, you are just a boy.
You played by your own rules.
Now you're sad, you want me back.
My dearest, pre-loved friend,
I want you to know I love you lots, you're just the best.
But you're never getting back to me.
Count to a million just for me,
And I'd still never be friends with you.
I'll accept your apology.
If you have changed from the boy into a man,
I'm proud of you.
But you had your chance, and now you're gone.
No second chance for a pre-loved friend.
Hey, what can I say?
You're just a pre-loved friend.

Playing Puddysticks

I want to go playing puddysticks.
I never found something so enjoyable.
Push and push, them to their limits, watch them break down.
I'm playing puddysticks, and it's all OK for me. I'm not in danger; they are in favour of taking me to the day of some, we say.
Come, now. It's just a game,
A puddysticks game.
Not ridiculous, just beating us.
One up on them, and they're slowly going down.
We're playing puddysticks, puddysticks chasing me.
Not puddysticks taking me,
Playing puddysticks, your game is too easy.
I've won already, and I didn't even need your instructions to win.

Rawky, I Love

Rawky, I love.
Come with me; I've got my time, my colours, and me
In the damp, and I say
I don't care about a bottom.
I don't mind, not seeing where I go.
And I don't mind you saying I'm so weird. I know what I'm doing.
You would never know, come when it does.
And you need Rawky, I love, but instead of being ready,
You'd die in a moment, I trust.
Rawky, I love.
Doesn't love you.
Didn't teach; now you're to be taught in an instant.
Rawky, I love,
Rawky, I love.
Such a special place.

Why Is Everyone a Screenager?

All of you, sitting in front of your computer screen,
Spending more time of your precious life.
You could try to sort out crime.
'Nah, I wanna play on my computer.'
Why is everyone a screenager?
Staring into a small abyss; it shows lies, it shows you distractions.
Why do you believe all the nonsense that the screenage brings?
Do you think it's better when everybody is watching you, what you do, and what you say?
I see it as a form of annoyance, brainwashing.
People talking doesn't exist—gotta hide behind a screen.
'I just can't resist.'
Why is everyone a screenager?

Could I Be a Shavetail?

You say I play superbly.
It's like a match, it's like a true player.
But what if it's bias?
What if it's all just pretend?
What if I have worked hours on end just to be lied to?
Could I be a shavetail?
Am I really that good? 'Cause I doubt that,
I think I know I doubt that.
You say it's just confidence.
You say to keep my face up.
But how can I face a spotlight if no spotlight's on me?
Could I be a shavetail?
Or is it just me?

I Find Myself a Superbious Match

I find myself a superbious match,
That, of course, being me.
I made my mind up long ago:
I am what is best for me and all those with me.
Nobody else, just me.
I am proud of who I am, what I know I am.
I'm proud of what I have become,
What I chose to be, and
I'll fight on the front line for my people.
I find myself a superbious match for my country,
For me, for family.
Glory where the wind blows,
When the wind stops we have won.
When the wind rages, we gather for the greatest attack against our enemies.
Outwit the opponent, for the battle is already over in an instant.
And when we start to lose, I find myself a superbious match and defeat them.
I found myself in my superbious matches.

My Velleity

My velleity, an idol,
But I don't have the strength to hold.
I want to be the best and adored,
But I don't have the guts to perform.
My friends all adore me, for heaven's sake.
I know that I am amazing, but I just can't
My veilleity.
I exhaust myself to practice all day,
But I can't push myself enough.
I'm such a fool, I'm just a tool.
What can I do with my velleity?
It's a wasted gift I want to give to someone else,
So they can have a go and enjoy what I can't.
But then I'd get jealous. My velleity is a waste, is it not?

I Hold to Myself Verjuice

I hold to myself verjuice,
In such delight do I taste a bitter.
Woven fabrics smell like liquor,
Make me feel depressed in the sunshine when everybody's having fun without me.
Sunshine in my day doesn't melt my heart like butter into a sweet aroma,
Rather burnt into ashes by the flames of the sun.
I hold to myself verjuice.
Grape will satisfy my thirst.
Takes my life into a green place,
A sweet and sour place.
Burn bright, I hide,
Make myself at home in the dim moonlight.
Silence is my favourite sound.
I turn my sweet music
Into sour, soft violins,
Sending me to sleep
On a cute dream.
I hold to myself verjuice.
Its taste is defined as me.

Heaven Calls My Name

I can play what you want,
I can act for so long.
I can dance with you; in a happy tune I stay.
For eternity if I may, I may not.
I can swallow all my fears as long as you are with me.
But what happens when you're gone?
I've gotta believe, gotta believe.
Stay strong; don't hurt me.
Angel,
I now know
What I could hear in my sleep,
And now I can hear it clearer than ever before, now that you are no longer covering my ears.
Heaven calls my name,
It calls me, and I follow.
I follow like a lost lamb to the slaughterhouse, but I'm holding the knife.
What is it now? You know
I have fallen to darkness.
Kept telling myself to be strong.
Did it work, ever?
Wondering where I would be without you.
Six feet underneath, hardly breathing, dying for believing.
Save me.
Angel,
I love you,
And now heaven's calling my name,

Wants to see me on the other side.
I don't want the blues to take me.
I don't want to live whilst nine must die—
Make it ten.
Leave me out, because I'm just bronze.
Third place only, taking up space for somebody else
On the pedestal.
Heaven's call.
My eyes are fading into the warm light.
Red milk covers me and what I need to be.
Love, love, I do it for love, I do it for you.
My wrists are open, diluted in the bath, I know.
Heaven's coming after me.
Is it my time?
Time, time.
I love you, and so I do this all for you.
When the chime falls to me,
I do what I must.
I slip as I bathe.
It'll only hurt for a little while.
But the bubbles will cover my face,
And the water sings its song.
The last of the bubbles fly to the highest peak alive.
My body begins to relax, softens in the bath.
The water is red, my eyes are closed, my lips are parted.
I'm singing a song in my head about the love, about the times when I wasn't dead.

It's undeniable I'll miss you so much,
But they all said it's best for me, the world's a better place without me.
So I lie stone cold, whiter by the second, I know.
I'm left in a red bath, and it embraces me, the final embrace of my time,
The last that I'll feel, the dying ember against my sore skin.
I thought that I was something else. Now my thoughts are clouded by the red of the sea, carrying me away on a night trail
Of eternity,
And I'm all still in my thoughts of heaven's call.
If you discover me tomorrow,
Then I'll tell you I love you today.
But only through this poem can I say
I'm in the way, and you're so much more.
Heaven calls my name.
Take me home,
In a place I finally belong.

Death to My Harmful Traits

My paintbrush is so sharp,
It cuts through any canvas.
And I try out different colours on my arms.
I make special little paintings,
Facing on my legs,
Down my neck, hesitant.
But it makes me feel so good inside.
Scarlet ribbons falling, dropping
Down my peach soft skin.
Paint it round my body.
Angels love me for who I am.
What I do,
It brings me happiness
Through the pain, the blur,
The savage confusion
In my mind.
My eyes
Can't seem to stop,
They beg to see
Red beauty.
Even now, it still holds me,
Binds my body,
Wraps me in the sulphur that'll kill me.
When I protest,
It silences me,
Treats me like a slave.
When I'm meant to enjoy it,

Death to my harmful traits!
I say,
But you can't get off me,
And I can't get off of you.
You're my special high.
I screamed for love,
But all they wanted was my money.
Pretend you shine the light so I can see,
Then jump away in your comfortable Ferrari.
Death to my harmful traits!
I can't live with this anymore,
Living wherever he goes,
Loving wherever she goes.
Take me to your darker side.
I change my life
To suit my changing, playing.
Guys thought they could go gaming, blaming.
Honey, me, we're saving, gaining
Illegally, with pain 'n' fame 'n' the city of the gazing.
Yes, I've got a cure.
No, it's not pure.
Wake me up when I bring
Death to my harmful traits!

Life Is Just so Beautiful without You

Life is just so beautiful without you,
Up upon the treasure chest.
Then you'll miss the gold, and
I'll have my diamonds
Shining, shining.
I'm finally feeling free.
The absence of your downpour has brought some sunshine in the day.
Just perhaps did I not know
There was a candle,
And life could be lit if you give it flame.
When you played your games,
You thought they'd last,
Like I'd play along.
Did you not consider
The possibility that I'd
Throw away and burn your game myself?
Oh, Mama said life is too precious.
It's a beautiful thing.
She was right:
Life is just so beautiful without you.
I could blame you for my bitter taste and
The cold, dark black that I wear in May, but
It wouldn't be true to my heart to say
That I'm still a child,
I haven't grown in any way.

Come and tell me
What was your favourite
Part of our time together?
Was it the part where you said you loved me?
Kissed me forever?
Now I look back at it, and could I ever
Bring my lips to touch yours?
Never,
Though it felt so good
To caress your hair.
It'll never be as beautiful
As the days I've spent without you.
Oh, well.
Life can be so much more than you,
It can be so much more than my dreams.
Because I'm finally in the driver's seat,
I'll speed through my enemies,
And I don't care what I do is wrong;
It feels so right to me.
My life doesn't matter,
It's not a factor.
With a thousand of my dreams came true,
All in the same night,
Life, oh beautiful,
Oh how free
Like the ocean,
As bright as I can possibly beam.

Life is just so beautiful without you.
I fell to my saviour,
And that saviour was me.
Oh, I'm alive.
Today, tomorrow, the next day,
I carry on, I carry on.
Because life,
Yes, life,
Is just so beautiful without you.
It's the best feeling in the world.
The ones that have always been with me
Are all I need
To be complete
In the unthawable ice in my heart,
Like the caps,
Staying forever.
Life is just so beautiful without you.
Stand next to me,
Tell me I'm the same
As the one you discovered outside the gates.

I Love You a Billion

Oh no—I feel the dread coming to me.
I feel a billion bullets penetrating me.
I could die,
But I don't want to die.
I don't want you to be sad when I'm happy.
Oh no, oh yes, oh no, oh yeah.
I love you a billion.
Don't try to deny
That I love you.
I love you beyond the ballads of time,
Stronger than the meteorites that'll destroy our earth.
I love you for all that you are,
Higher than the mountain of Everest.
I love you, I love you, I love you,
I love you a billion.
Oh-ho, I know the crime of care,
But I can pack a billion crimes and the sentence of eternal life.
I could breathe in the water,
But I don't want to never be heard,
I don't want to never be heard.
I don't want you to cry when I smile.
Oh, oh, oh, yeah.
Let's not cry; I lose my sight
When you are not happy.
Happy, I want to be happy
Forever and ever.

I love you a billion,
I love you.
Oh, God, I could reach your heavens if you tried to measure my love
For the one.
You are the one.
I won't hide what I feel
For you.
I love you a billion.
Now do you love me?
Do you strike, love?
Can you compare me
To anyone you know?
Power, power, to you.
Oh, power!
Power for you, a billion I own.
Hold me closely as I fly in my heart.
Cream pastel covers us,
It holds us.
Oh, honey, you smell like sweet honey.
Oh, I love you a billion.
Take me to the star show;
I'll take you to your favourite restaurant.
Honey, oh honey,
Don't be sad
Because you love me,
And that's all I need.

I love you a billion,
And I know you're wanting me.
Struggle to the top.
Oh, we're never going to drop.

I'm Invincible

I'm invincible,
And I don't need your baby steps
To bring me up.
I'm going to take a leap off the mountains
And trust in God that I'll be all right.
I make my decisions right away;
I'm a dandelion, I'm everywhere.
I fall so far,
I hold my head up high.
I'm invincible, I'm invincible,
And you cannot beat me.
Said you'd show me the way,
But I have sight, and I will stay,
You say anyone can write.
Oh, no? Well, guess what?
I can write fantastic,
I can write every single day,
Love what I do.
I love you too,
Because you give me something to write about.
And I don't mind if you beg I'm crazy.
Yes, your poor words can't bring me down,
And your old threats are out of town,
But I am sticking to the sound.
Call me crazy because I've got books stacked on my head,
and I'm calling it a crown!
I'm invincible.

Your apologies are too late.
You don't mean them—the attention,
You want attention.
Here's your attention:
I love me, and I'll always be happy.
I have soft rays of light shining upon me.
I love me,
I love me!
I'm invincible! I'm invincible!
Every stone, every carving,
Every penny, every farthing.
I'm invincible! I'm invincible!
God, I'm invincible!
I found my confidence
Hidden deep down inside me!
It's released!
Oh, I love myself
Forever, forever, ever forever, ever, forever, forever, ever.
I found the one,
That I love the most.
My confidence is strong,
Selfishness is raw.
I'm powerful!
I'm colourful!
I'm invincible!
Yes, I'm invincible!
Pour down the glass

To our merry side, that's free.
Make our minds fall prey to their imaginings.
May I, may I?
I may create the most beautiful picture ever.
I mean what I say.
Let our cheeks burn beetroot red,
Set the fireworks alight,
Watch them explode!
Big, bad bikers burning through the flames!
Firing guns, bullets enter the sky.
Wear my flag with pride,
Because I am proud,
Proud of all, proud of me …
Pride to myself and I'm!
Invincible! Invincible! I'm invincible! Invincible!
May I? I may scream tonight,
Get into a fight with my crew.
I love 'em all,
I love me.
I! Am! Invincible! I! Am! Invincible! I am! I am invincible!
I'm invincible!
And no one is breaking me down tonight!
No, not ever,
For I am,
I'm invincible!

I Now Know My Name

I always stood in the water, all alone,
Bare feet cool and toes curling for long.
Walking on the stones of timelessness;
They scream an emerald green,
Being washed away by the trickling of the earth's veins.
I'm still learning
About the love, about the sorrow.
I'm still trying.
When I was losing myself to the demons
And the sky was falling on me,
I could have coiled myself into a ball,
Forgotten who I am.
I, I,
I now know my name!
Just like Constable—he found his name in his day!
He painted pictures for us to admire beauty.
I paint pictures for us to understand beauty.
I found my own friends,
So fantastical we have adventures every day.
I can love my own life,
Dance to the rhythm of your
Cold insults,
Green eyes staring into my window.
Oh, sorrow—which guess what? I don't miss!

I'll fight like a lion.
I'm a beast with passion,

The king of his army,
The army he fights for,
Dies for.
And they would do the same.
Power to my people because they are the greatest.
They lifted me until my talons could beat the sky,
Soaring the scapes,
Iron in my bones,
Electric in my eyes.
Let's defeat all the performances today.
I now know my name!
Just like Dyson, he gave originality in his bagless hoover, brilliant inventions and persevered.
I give originality as a twenty-first-century boy.
I'll never stop persevering.
I am Cameron McNaughton!
I am the greatest!
The mistakes I made were rectified.
I can build the secure kingdom.
I can breed a storm of such immense mass.
I now know my name!
Like Nelson with the cannon,
His weapon,
Discipline his lifestyle.
He found his name.
My pen, my weapon.
Discipline my words in paper.

It's my best name!
The best!
You guys, you never broke me.
You only gave me the power of the earth.
You believed you could drown me in your pearls of lies.
Well, you believed.
Just look into my eyes!

I can prep to my heart's content.
I can free myself.
I can be who I am.
I'm free, I'm free.
I now know my name!
Like Bernard Matthews, I stand tall.
Don't be afraid because you start small.
He was a van driver
Who hatched into legend,
His work a '*bootiful*' inspiration to me,
To innovate and carry on
With my poetry.
I'm Cameron, I'm Cameron, Cameron McNaughton!
I'm the twenty-first-century child of the world,
Just like Shakespeare.
I'll test my limits and my love for literature;
I want it to feel as alive as his,
Always aim for my best self.

I am what I know I am!
Running from who I am
Is just mental suicide.
So I'll dance faster
In the dirt, in the sand,
On the stage, and with my band.
My pen glides across the page in the most enthusiastic fashion.
I look towards the light.
I'm alive.
My pen,
I brandish it.
I now know my name!
My name is Cameron McNaughton!
I'm a proud McNaughton.
I am powerful,
I am unstoppable.
I'm Cameron McNaughton,
I am happy,
I am confident in who I am.
I now know my name.
Now you know it too!

Lightning Source UK Ltd.
Milton Keynes UK
UKHW012013110419
340890UK00001B/13/P